The *Ars Typographica* Library
General Editor: James Moran

ERIC GILL
THE MAN WHO LOVED LETTERS

Uniform with this volume
Allen Hutt: Fournier
Leslie Owens: J. H. Mason

ERIC GILL

THE MAN WHO LOVED LETTERS

ROY BREWER

LONDON : FREDERICK MULLER LTD : 1973

To my wife

FIRST PUBLISHED 1973 BY
FREDERICK MULLER LTD
110 FLEET STREET LONDON EC4A 2AP

COPYRIGHT © ROY BREWER 1973

DESIGNED BY CRAIG DODD

PRINTED AND BOUND IN GREAT BRITAIN BY
COX & WYMAN LTD
LONDON, FAKENHAM AND READING

ISBN 0 584 10351 4

CONTENTS

ACKNOWLEDGEMENTS

I am indebted to many sources for help and information, particularly to James Moran, the editor of this series of monographs, John Dreyfus of The Monotype Corporation, and to Douglas Cleverdon who kindly supplied me with the full transcripts of recorded interviews relating to Eric Gill. Other sources are acknowledged in the text, but I would like to mention particularly Robert Harling's article "The Type Designs of Eric Gill", which appeared in the typographical journal *Alphabet and Image* (January 1948) which Mr Harling then edited. This provided a most valuable and comprehensive source of information on Gill's types as well as Mr Harling's own perceptive and informed commentary. Also of great value has been the extensive essay "Eric Gill als Schriftkünstler" by Wolfgang Kehr which appeared in *Archiv für Geschichte des Buchwesens*, Vol IV, editions 2 and 3. My thanks are due to William E. Conway of the Andrew Clark Memorial Library, Los Angeles, California, USA, for permission to use the illustration on page 25, to Florian J. Shasky, the Special Collections Librarian of the Richard A. Gleeson Library at the University of San Francisco for permission to use the drawing on page 2, and to the Publicity Department of London Transport for supplying the broadsheet reproduced on page 54. Thanks are also due to Miss Sandra Raphael for the compilation of the index.

LIST OF ILLUSTRATIONS

FOREWORD

There is no shortage of published material on or by Eric Gill, a man inclined to write on any subject which moved him, and one who appeared to the public of his day to be even more eccentric than was expected of "artists". The stories about him, some no doubt apocryphal, relating to his clothes, his rows with ecclesiastics, his attitude to the human body and to sex have been in circulation for many years, and it could be maintained that there was hardly a need for another book on this colourful figure.

But, as Roy Brewer points out ". . . it is sometimes necessary to remind oneself that Gill's greatest accomplishments were not literary, but graphic", and it is more important today to turn aside from the political, religious and social controversies in which Gill was involved and actually look at the work of a major master craftsman.

His works in stone are dispersed over a wide area and although they can be studied in photographs and in reproductions in books they should really be seen at first hand, which involves travelling. His illustrations are more readily available for study if the books can be obtained, but of all his productions the most ubiquitous and yet, to the uninitiated, the most anonymous are his typefaces.

This book is about those creations which, though based on traditional sources and manufactured in quantity, are worthy of the name. Paradoxically, Gill was originally one of those who were opposed to mass production, and, if anything, printing is not only a mass production process, but was one of the earliest in history. Actually, as Roy Brewer points out, Gill may not have been as uncompromising as his writings imply, but he still needed to be persuaded that his drawn or incised letters should be turned into pieces of type by an industrial process.

Here the hand of the entrepreneur, Stanley Morison, becomes apparent. Morison was no artist, but he could inspire artists and, just as important for the improvements of standards of printing, could persuade business men that certain type faces were commercially necessary and that men such as Gill should design them.

While this book is a record and evaluation of Gill's typefaces, the author has also provided a background against which they need to be considered – the technical aspects of type manufacture, the Roman alphabet, and the art of typography; much of it permeated with Gill's philosophical outlook.

Gill, it is true, had experimented with type design as early as 1917, but it was really only after Morison's skilled advocacy that he began designing in 1925 for The Monotype Corporation – afterwards he designed for others besides the Corporation. One type he designed for himself, although this is now available in the Monotype range. Another ended up as a Linotype face.

Much in the history of type design and manufacture is obscure and confusing. Roy Brewer has not only provided a perceptive analysis of Gill's typefaces, but has also recorded their provenance, a valuable contribution in itself.

In time, the controversies in which Gill took part will be forgotten and his stonework may be worn away; but the best of his typefaces will endure, not only set in books in public and private libraries, but stored, as it were, in matrices, whether incised or on film and in ways yet unknown, since alphabetic characters which combine to form a readable and harmonious whole will always be needed, however advanced the technique for composing and printing.

JAMES MORAN

ERIC GILL
1882–1940

THIS IS NOT A BIOGRAPHY OF ERIC GILL; IT CONCENTRATES on a relatively small sector of his output and one which occupied only the later part of his working life. It is an unsatisfactory approach for those who want to know more about Gill the man than about the twenty-six letters to which he dedicated so much of his time. But, as James Moran has said "there is no shortage of published material on or by Eric Gill" and it is this fact which must be my main excuse for not repeating it. Those whose curiosity makes them want to know more about Gill may satisfy it with his own *Autobiography* and with Robert Speaight's admirable *The Life of Eric Gill* (Methuen; 1966). The former is revealing (sometimes, it would seem, unintentionally); the work of a man who, in spite of his honesty and forthrightness, was not well-equipped for dispassionate self-analysis. Speaight's biography is a painstaking, well-rounded portrait which makes perceptive use of what Gill said and wrote and what his associates and friends thought about him and about the things he did. It is Gill on the "wide screen" which suited his personality.

As befits a controversialist, Gill came in for a good deal of praise and blame during his lifetime and immediately after his death. He also earned – even courted – some uncritical adulation by playing the part of the prophet and soothsayer when it suited him. He liked having disciples. But, maybe because many of the burning issues he raised have cooled or maybe because Gill was not always a very convincing or consistent prophet, his dominating presence, once removed, was quickly dimmed and diminished in retrospect.

For present purposes, the reader must be content with a mere outline of Gill's life, yet bear in mind that it was a varied and eventful one which Gill lived to the full, never tiring of "trying things out" and of striving towards a lifestyle which he felt in his bones to be the one which would allow man to retain his faculties, his dignity and, above all, his responsibility to others in the face of threats by the modern world to curtail all three.

Arthur Eric Rowton Gill was born in Brighton in 1882, the second of thirteen children. His father was an Assistant Minister to the Chapel of the Countess of Huntingdon's Connexion in North Street. By the age of fifteen, during a schooling without academic distinction, he was already displaying a talent for drawing and an instinct for nicely-judged proportions. He was fascinated by machinery and, particularly, by railway engines. John Dreyfus showed me a little drawing, which Gill did when he was about fourteen years old, of an engine and, apart from its neatness and skill for a young boy of that age, the lettering on the side of the locomotive foreshadows Gill's feeling for the spatial relationship of letters, one to another, and to their surroundings.

He was apprenticed to the architect of the Ecclesiastical Commissioners in 1900 but, three years later, left his apprenticeship and, already having studied lettering with Edward Johnston at evening classes, started his own business as a letter-cutter and monumental mason. Many commissions for inscriptional lettering followed. He was married in 1904 to Ethel Mary Moore and, in

A drawing made by Gill when aged about 10. Note the precocious lettering on the side of the engine

1907, moved to Ditchling in Sussex where, as a member of a community of craftsmen, he worked with others of like mind and spirit. Here he obtained his first practical experience of printing on a hand-press, and of the techniques and disciplines of typography, though his own contribution to Hilary Pepler's St Dominic's Press at Ditchling was mainly illustrations in the form of wood-cuts and initial letters.

Gill was received into the Catholic Church on his thirty-first birthday and, thereafter, was an ardent Catholic. He left Ditchling in 1924 and moved to a remote place in the Black Mountains of mid-Wales, Capel-y-ffin. Shortly afterwards he met Stanley Morison and commenced his work on type design for The Monotype Corporation, parallel with his other activities as a sculptor, lettering artist, stone carver and wood engraver.

He had three daughters, Perpetua, Joanna and Felicity, all of whose names he used for naming his own typefaces.

In 1928 he left Capel-y-ffin and moved to a farm at High Wycombe called Piggotts, where he re-established his studio and stone-cutting workshop. There was probably no considerable part of his life in which he was concerned solely, or even mainly, with type design. His work on types sprang naturally from his love of letters and, as we shall see, it sometimes conflicted with the different set of disciplines he had learned and developed as a letter-cutter in wood and stone. But his religion and his temperament urged him to grapple with every problem which his special skills might help to solve, and there was in Gill, as someone who knew him remarked to me, an over-riding factor which he derived from his religious beliefs: that we are in the world to work, and work hard; that, in the end, we may each be called upon by God to account in detail for what we have done. This may help to explain Gill's relentless energy; his determination to get things right and to meet every challenge which arose. He was taken ill early in 1940 and died of lung cancer on 17 November of that year.

Nameplate cut by Gill: he rarely used his initials, but did so on this occasion

I

WHO WAS ERIC GILL?

The only reason for writing anything is to answer one's own questions. In the process of finding the answers, however incomplete or provisional, you might answer someone else's questions. (*Stanley Morison*)

ONE OF ERIC GILL'S COLLECTIONS OF ESSAYS IS CALLED It *All Goes Together*. This title expresses a basic tenet of Gill's life and work and is a guide to anyone who wishes to understand either. "Integrity", in its commonly accepted moral sense, and in its more precise definition "all of a piece", is a word which crops up again and again when people write or talk about Gill. It is doubtful whether he himself would have admitted even the distinction between "life" and "work" which I have already made. So, to write about him as a designer of types is to risk, at best, a false focus and, at worst, a complete distortion of his approach to the designing of printing types. Gill was, as the Victorians liked to say of such people, "a man of many parts" and, in his case, the parts fitted together with extraordinary precision.

It is to Gill's consistency rather than to his versatility as a writer-teacher-sculptor-designer-artist-printer *et al* that we should look in any attempt to discover what he did and why he did it in his own particular way. A Gill typeface on the page tells us a little, but not much, about the concepts which motivated its creation; less today than it would have done forty years ago when Gill types stood in sharper distinction from the commercial commonplace. In type design Gill incorporated the ideas which he preached and practised in other spheres – the human need for dignity and beauty as integral with what is useful and as part of the whole thing, not merely added embellishments.

In some ways, however, it is easier to write about Gill's type designs than it would be to investigate other aspects of his creative output. Gill wrote quite a lot about typography and we have plenty of other informed opinions and assessments on which to draw.

It is as well to remember that purely typographical judgements do not go very far or very usefully into the reasons why certain types came into being or why they were successful. That is why a great deal of what follows is concerned not only with Gill's type designs but also with lettering, type-founding and typographic design in general.

There was a time when Gill himself had to find out what type was for and what it could and could not do on a page. Having done so he applied himself industriously and successfully to the practicalities of its design. In the work of this one man we have a synthesis of the historical development of letter-ing, from the incised inscription via the pen formed letter to metal type as used for printing. Until he started designing types Gill had a purely hand-craftsman's conception of lettering and of design in general. He was con-stantly making distinctions between "good design", by which he meant sound craft practices, and "commercial opportunism" as evinced in mass produc-tion. He did not enjoy things which were "apart from nature" though he included in "nature" many things including, eventually, the nature of urban society and its artefacts!

By the time he had started to design types Gill had moved from the extreme position he had taken earlier in relation to "mass produced objects" (of which type is one) and was no longer ready to condemn anything and everything which was not the product of a man's own hands. It is open to question whether Gill was ever as uncompromising about this as his writings imply. He was not the sort of man to opt out of an argument; indeed, if there was not an argument going he started one. He enjoyed convincing people and knew that, to convince them, it was necessary sometimes to sur-prise and intrigue them. His prime concern was practical improvement as, for example, was his attitude to dress. While Gill's own dress was thought by some to be eccentric it was, in fact, suited to his idea of comfort, freedom and convenience and his objection to conventional attire — "Our clothes are a mass of foolish gadgets" -- was well-founded. He recognized the influence which people in the public eye could have and was not shy of being in the limelight.

So Gill talked and wrote indefatigably, his writing revealing the enthusiasm with which he rushed to meet each new challenge, sometimes inadequately equipped to face it. In his work this vitality was controlled and disciplined by the medium. His woodcuts, engravings and drawings show this in their freedom within carefully planned and meticulously observed spatial relation-ships. Such care and control have a close link with the disciplines of type design.

It is no longer fashionable to use the word "humanistic" to describe that which springs from a specifically human awareness of what is pleasing and proper for people, but it has always been the humanistic factor which divides good work from the merely adequate. Gill made this point, from a somewhat different premise, when he wrote in an essay, "Those things we call secular which, though not irreligious, do not envisage God as their end immediately. Thus a church is called a religious building, and an inn we call secular. But an inn is not therefore irreligious"

He knew perfectly well the differences between those who created and those who made use of the creations of others and, while he refused to place the maker apart from the people for whom he worked, he insisted that the designer should always be the maker and that those who wanted beautiful things should "win the right to make them for themselves and allow that right to others". To some degree this view is idealistic, but at least it emphasizes the active involvement of the designer: it abolishes the ivory tower and puts him into the workshop, which is the best place for him.

From a contemporary standpoint it may be easier to agree with what Gill was trying to say than it was earlier in this century. We are now less unnerved by the terms on which we obtain the fruits of mass production or maybe we are more conditioned to accepting them without question.

For all this it must have been hard to focus the energies of a man like Gill on the production procedures of typefounding on a commercial scale and to feed and sustain these energies. It was Stanley Morison, then typographic adviser to The Monotype Corporation, who did so in ways which only he knew how. Beatrice Warde, one of Morison's colleagues at Monotype, in a talk to the Double Crown Club, spoke of the period during which Gill and Morison collaborated. "During all that time" she said, "Morison was behind him helping and making things possible, caring very much that Gill should do what he liked." Of course when some people do what they like the result is valuable, and Gill was one of these. Mrs Warde said that Morison was "the only living man" who could have brought about the change in Gill's career which prompted him to undertake type design at a time when he was already happy and successful in other fields. The fact that Gill liked an argument and Morison was always ready to give him one probably had something to do with it; this, and the tenacity which Gill could show when pursuing a new activity, proved productive.

It was typical of Gill's extrovert personality that, as soon as he was sure of himself in the field of type design, he wrote a book about typography in which he suggested that a lot of people had been wrong about a lot of things

DUKE OF YORK'S THEATRE

CHARLES FROHMAN PRESENTS

QUALITY STREET

By J. M. BARRIE

THE VOYSEY INHERITANCE

By H. GRANVILLE BARKER

STRIFE

By JOHN GALSWORTHY

MAJOR BARBARA

By BERNARD SHAW

THE REPERTORY THEATRE

Lettering drawn for a theatre and matched, on this bill, with Caslon text

until he came along to put them right. To sympathize with this crusading and, to those who prefer understatement, somewhat bellicose readiness to join issue with the pundits, one must look further than Gill's writings on typography. When he died in 1940, aged fifty-eight, he had spent thirty-two years during which he was hardly ever out of the public arena. He had what seems an almost compulsive need to share his opinions, prejudices, beliefs and reactions with other people. Whether what he wrote and said was of public interest at the time did not seem to matter so much as the fact that it was said quickly and forcefully. Essays, letters, pamphlets, articles, hand-books – Gill's restless and often scolding pen was ready to teach, praise, persuade, advise, cajole and reflect on subjects as disparate as birth-control, sculpture, dress, a ride on the Flying Scotsman, money, cathedrals, morals and carols. With all this in view it is sometimes necessary to remind oneself that Gill's greatest accomplishments were not literary, but graphic.

Evan Gill's *Bibliography* of his brother's written work, published by Cassell in 1953, must surely be the most entrancing example of this sort of scholarly compilation. It is generously illustrated with ninety-six facsimiles of title pages and contains designs and devices executed in various media. Here we may see that, though Gill was a prolific and even garrulous commentator on the contemporary scene, he was economical to the point of austerity with chisel, brush and pen. In the collection of drawings, rubbings, templates, proofs and sketches containing some 2,000 items acquired from Gill's widow and preserved by The Monotype Corporation one can get a good idea of what Gill was best at doing: the style is coolly authoritative, the line sensitive and precise, the work of a man who had solved graphic problems with the right tools used intelligently; a man who could back what he said about letters with the work of hand and eye. So we do not need to take on trust what Gill has said about himself, or what others have written about the quality of the work of this artist-craftsman. It can be evaluated today, perhaps more thoroughly than it could have been in his own time.

I chose Gill as the subject of this book when James Moran told me of his plan for a series of monographs on the typographic arts and invited me to contribute. It was foolhardy, perhaps, to expect to be able to say anything new about a man who said so much about himself and who has received such careful attention from knowledgeable contemporaries and successors. But I was persuaded to think that a book about Gill as a type-designer would not be superfluous if only because this facet of Gill's creative output has received less attention than others. In type design and typography there is a constant need to renew acquaintance with what is used, often without thought; to look again

ART NONSENSE
AND OTHER ESSAYS
BY ERIC GILL

LONDON
CASSELL & CO., LTD. & FRANCIS WALTERSON
1929

Sensitive letterspacing
and the elegance of
Perpetua in a title page
for a collection of Gill's
essays, the first book
using this typeface. The
wood engraving is also
by Gill.

at letter forms and, occasionally, to revise our original thoughts about them. Familiarity with types breeds indifference, and indifference is the enemy of perceptiveness.

Gill's name crops up frequently in books about printing and typography but usually only as a passing reference. Robert Speaight's admirable biography, The Life of Eric Gill (Methuen, 1966) deals but incidentally with Gill's type designs, and Gill's intensely subjective Autobiography is, for the most part, busy with other matters.

Yet, in their way, Gill's typefaces are the most easily accessible examples of his skill as a craftsman in letters. They are still being used in the ways in which Gill wanted them to be used – for the good and beauty of things. This book is set in 11 point Joanna type.

Gill did not design any types that were cut until around 1925, but there is evidence that he had given thought to the problems of type design before that. The results of his work in the type field depended, more than in any other of his graphic activities, on his relationship and collaboration with people who were professionally concerned with the production of printing types. To this extent a book about Gill's types must take notice of the opinions of such people as Morison, Mrs Warde and Robert Harling, as well as of other, less eminent, people who are as anonymous today as they were when they applied themselves to the transformation of Gill's drawings into metal type characters.

So the challenge is to make an up-to-date evaluation of Gill's work in type design, and to do so from a contemporary standpoint. To discover, for example, how accurate was his diagnosis of what the printing industry most needed from the type designer in the 1920s and 30s. Remember that he reacted to conditions and standards of everyday commercial printing which were different from and, most people would agree, lower than today's average, and some of the things he said and did then can now seem over-stressed or wide of the mark. Yet it was Gill, and people like him, who did much to re-establish decent standards of design in type and typography wherever they could. The standards, it should be said, were not just their opinions of what was good and bad but the products of a long-standing traditions of graphic excellence which, because occasionally mislaid by ignorance, fashion, ineptitude or greed, needed constant rediscovery.

Anyone who just reads Gill's articles and essays about typography might expect him to be a revolutionary in his practices and style. No doubt he thought of himself in this way. But a sight of Gill's letter-cutting and type design shows him to be more a conservative. It is probable that, early in this century, such regard as Gill had for the truths and traditions of his crafts was indeed "revolutionary" to those who were used to making a facile distinction between "art" and "industry". Gill would have none of this.

He was not, however, internationally-minded. Whether or not he knew or cared much about what was going on abroad, he rarely looked beyond the immediate situation for his inspiration. He did not seem to care whether things were being ordered more to his liking in America, or in the rest of Europe. The zesty breezes which blew across the typographic scene of the 1920s and 30s from Switzerland and Germany left him unruffled. It was not hard for him to appear a shocker, a goad or a mentor at home: Gill was fighting different battles from those of *Die Neue Typographie.* On the other hand Gill may well have had influence in Europe. The title pages which he and Edward Johnston did for Count Harry Kessler's Insel Verlag series of German classics are said to have been instrumental in weaning some German typographers away from their habit of using blackletter and turning them to the refinements of the roman alphabet in its purer form.

Gill was no medievalist. He was (and his friends confirm this) a truly "modern" man, and would have been the first to scoff at William Morris's view of London as potentially "small, white and clean". He wrote savagely about "art nonsense" (which we might now call "arty nonsense") and, were he still alive, would probably have had equally sharp things to say about "art-and-industry nonsense". The merely fashionable bored and irritated him. He wanted to go deeper. "The point", he says in his *Autobiography*, "is that the whole world has got it firmly fixed in its head that the object of working is to obtain as large an amount of material goods as possible, and that with the increased application of science and the increased use of machinery, that amount will be very large indeed, while at the same time the amount of necessary labour will become less and less until, machines being minded by machines, it will be almost none at all." This, he warned, was "dangerous nonsense", and surely he was right.

In the following pages I shall take whatever advantages hindsight offers. It may not always be enough to say what Gill wrote, said or did. We must ask whether the lessons he taught and the examples he gave have stood the test of time.

In type design and typography Gill was not an original thinker. He learned from others, and learned well, though his style of expression is unmistakable when he expresses a typographical opinion. His work with Stanley Morison and the people at The Monotype Corporation was an expansion of his own experience of lettering and, to a great degree, he remained firmly rooted in the classic tradition of letter-cutting, even when designing types which came to be used widely in commercial printing. He was neither too proud, nor too sure of himself, never to change his mind but, when he felt like it and knew that something important was at stake, Gill nailed his colours firmly to the mast. Was the fight worth while then? Has it been won?

Is Eric Gill now just a figure from the immediate past, of interest to art historians, typophiles and similar eclectics but of little importance to the everyday world of print? How well can our own views stand up to Gill's robust assertions? Even if the answers to such questions are vague or unsatisfactory, they are too interesting to neglect.

2

TYPEFOUNDING

FOR MOST PURPOSES IT IS SUFFICIENT TO JUDGE TYPE ON ITS appearance in the printed page – in reality the *image* which the actual type produces after inking and impression. But to remember that type is, strictly speaking, an artefact serves to focus attention on some useful points. The typefoundry is a factory for making types and it has to operate within the limitations imposed by the mechanics of production. The type designer may not get far if he works in ignorance of the ways in which type is made and, though he may wish to ignore them and give himself the freedom of the scribe or letter-cutter, the moment comes when a type design has to be measured to the mechanical requirements of modern typefounding and also to the mechanical limitations inherent in automatic typesetting machinery.

So far as the letterpress printing process is concerned these requirements are well-defined and fairly easily understood: there are things which a type designer may draw on paper which are demonstrably not workable if the drawings are to be used to create a character in a Monotype or Linotype matrix. Gill said of his Joanna type that "it was not designed to facilitate machine punch-cutting", but this did not mean that he was ignorant of the demands which punch-cutting machines make on a design. He had already encountered and learned much from his earlier collaboration with the people at The Monotype Corporation. His first well-known typeface, Perpetua, had brought Gill into contact with mentors and, as Beatrice Warde commented (*Commercial Art and Industry* No 12, 1932), "Gill knew he had something to learn: not how to cut punches skilfully, but how to put critical intelligence and technical precision to the normalizing of a type face by making sure that it would not distract the arm-chair reader by any detail that would look fussy and arbitrary on the printed book page."

When Gill was not preaching to the uninitiated he could approach the subject of type design with a touching humility as when he wrote to Stanley Morison apropos his drawn alphabets for Perpetua, "I expressly disclaimed the suggestion that I was type designing. I did not, and do not even now, profess to know enough about it." Yet, in the same letter, the Gill confidence returns and he says, ". . . I am coming round by degrees to consider myself capable of designing a fount of type." So he was – "by degrees", for in *The Fleuron* (No 7, 1930) Gill had written of his Perpetua type; "[The] drawings were not made as being specially suitable for printing type but simply as letters – letters as normal as might be according to my experience as a letter-cutter in stone and a painter of signs. To Mr Morison and the Monotype Corporation belongs the credit for making useful and presentable typefaces from them. Perpetua is a typographic version of an inscription letter. . . ."

What are the mysteries which Gill once called "typographical exigencies"? What are the differences between the free letter of the lettering artist and the "contained" letter of the modern type designer and why do they exist? To answer these questions a short digression into the making of printing types is necessary. It is easier to evaluate that which Gill, and other type designers, achieved if the mechanics of typefounding are taken into account. The reader who knows them already will, I hope, bear with the following short description, or skip it.

Gutenberg's invention was not printing: impressions from raised or incised surfaces had been printed long before Gutenberg's time, but it was he, by most accounts, who devised the materials and, above all, the adjustable mould for casting "moveable type"; that is type made of separate letters cast in metal which can be assembled and, with spacing and other materials, form a page of text from which, after inking, an impression may be taken. Thereafter the letters can be returned to the type cases (distributed, or "dissed" as the printer says) for further use.

Originally the punch, matrix and mould were needed to produce type from molten metal. The making of the punch was the most critical operation and the one demanding the greatest skill because the drawn letter had to be engraved accurately in hard metal in the same size as the piece of type which it would eventually produce. There are very few people today who can cut punches. Gill never attempted to do so and, though his first printing type, Perpetua, was hand-cut by one of the master punch-cutters of the day, Charles Malin, this may have been ordered by Morison more as a practical demonstration to impress Gill with the "handcraft" aspect of typefounding than from any inadequacy in the mechanical methods of punch-cutting in use by The Monotype Corporation. It should be noted that a fount of type in a particular size needs to be cut so that each character occupies an exactly calculated position in relation to all the other characters in the fount.

When types were hand-cut and hand-cast the punch was struck into a copper blank which formed the matrix into which molten type metal was poured in a mould which produced a piece of type of the required dimensions for printing.

The principle is not difficult to grasp, but it was some time before an alloy of metals was found which gave the needed characteristics for casting accurately, and the necessary durability for use as a printing surface. This, and the adjustable mould, were, in essence, Gutenberg's discovery.

In the same sense that a modern letterpress printing machine is a mechanized method of carrying out the sequence of operations which earlier

Typecasting by hand. From Moxon's "Mechanick Exercises" (1683–6), an early manual on printing and typefounding

printers used on their hand-presses – the positioning of the paper, inking of the forme, impression and removal of the printed sheet – the procedure followed by the early typefounders was eventually mechanized, both for the creation of type matrices and for automatic typecasting. The important difference between old and new methods of punch-cutting is the use of the pantograph. This device allows the letter to be engraved, at a predetermined scale of reduction, from an enlarged metal pattern on to the punch face.

The best description of modern punch-cutting I have seen is that given in The Monotype Recorder of September–October 1932, a special issue which dealt with Times New Roman type and its production. Stanley Morison's article on the designing and cutting of the type and the making of the matrices states, "The first step in manufacturing . . . was to take the finished drawing, and, by means of a projecting machine, to secure a true version of the original design, enlarged to 10 inches. This outline is drawn upon a prepared sheet lined in relation to a factor standardising the respective positions of the lower-case letters with each other and with their capitals. This precise pattern is next placed in a pantograph, which transfers a reduced copy of the design to a wax-coated glass plate. As the shape of this wax plate is outlined only, the 'body' of the design remaining between the outline, constituting its form, is removed. The plate is washed with silver nitrate and an electrotype taken. The electro shell being ready, it is backed, according to the usual practice of the trade, to produce the perfect metal pattern from which the punch is made. The punch-cutting machine also carries a pantograph, but, unlike the horizontal one used for transferring the paper pattern to the wax, is perpendicular in principle. The lower end of the punch-cutting pantograph is operated to follow the outline of the metal pattern, while the upper end works a small tool, moving at many revolutions a second, which cuts into the steel a reduced working of the pattern below. The process is a gradual one, in which the material at the end of the steel body of the punch is cut away until the character is completed. The machine, known as the Pierpont punch-cutting machine, works to the accuracy of one twenty-five-thousandth part of an inch, and produces punches from 4 point to 72 point."

The article goes on to describe the production of the matrix, which is used in the caster for the production of the actual type used in printing. In all essential details, the method of punch-cutting described by Morison was that used at the time when Gill's types were being cut.

Automatic composing machines use letter matrices instead of punches. In the case of machines made made by The Monotype Corporation, the matrices are within a type-casting machine separate from that on which the setting is keyboarded: the keyboard produces a punched paper roll which is used to control the caster. The operating principle of the Monotype requires the letter matrix to be in a single piece so that it can be moved mechanically, bringing the required letter into position for casting, When so positioned, the type metal is forced up through the mould against the matrix and, thus, as in the hand mould, a complete piece of type is formed. Other automatic composing machinery works from separate brass matrices and the type is moulded as a single piece of metal, line by line, which printers call "slugs" but the basic principle by which the letters are cast is very similar to that already described.

Such automatic casting as part of mechanical composition places physical limitations on the number and size of letters which can be accommodated in a single matrix.

It is customary to print mechanical setting once only. The setting is not "dissed", and the type metal is remelted and recast. This is one of the differences between type in machine-setting and the founder's type that more closely resembles the type of Gutenberg and his successors, being set by hand from typecases. Type which has been founded in this traditional manner enjoys a greater freedom from machine-imposed design limitations but, of course, the methods of setting are not those likely to be found in a modern printing factory with a large typesetting requirement.

Even from the above resumé it will be seen that there are essential differences between designing letters for typefounding and their cutting into a surface such as wood or stone with all the freedom this implies. Type has to be capable of being set as continuous text, and the letters must be able to be combined and re-combined to a fixed scheme which delimits their spatial relationships. Some letters – w and m for example – are wider than others, such as i and l, and the typographical factor of a typeface's "set width" comes into force. The hand-lettering artist may achieve subtle variations by deliberately expanding or condensing some letters, varying letter, word and line spacing, and using other spatial adjustments the better to attain a harmonious result. Type must be treated as type – as pieces of metal – and the designer forgets this at his peril.

Gill was no doubt made aware of it by his contact with Morison and by what he saw on his visits to the Monotype works at Salfords. Without such knowledge, his designs might never have seen the light of day, and the fact that they did shows how intelligently and co-operatively he worked in the new medium. This need not imply that Gill was ready to compromise: some of his most felicitous letters are the result of his asking "Why not?". His attitude to the job was, perhaps, analogous to that of a composer of music who sometimes makes what may be thought to be unreasonable technical demands on performers but who demonstrates that talented and dedicated people can often do what was formerly thought impossible, if it can be shown that the effort is worth while; techniques are expanded by such challenges.

Casting type. From Mackellar's "American Printer" (1889)

3

THE ROMAN ALPHABET
FROM STONE TO METAL

THE DIFFERENCE BETWEEN THE ROMAN LETTERS ENCOUNTERED
in printing types and incised letters, as used for monumental and
other inscriptions, is a subtle one. Gill was a master of the incised
letter, which he cut in stone, wood and other materials, many
examples of which remain as a testimony of his skill. It was because of his
abilities as a letter-cutter that Stanley Morison, then typographic adviser to
The Monotype Corporation, approached Gill with a view to getting him to
design a type but, up to this time, it is safe to say that Gill's interests and
activities in the lettering field had been concentrated mostly within the
considerably different disciplines of inscriptional lettering. In 1924 when
Morison wrote to Gill inviting him to contribute an article to *The Fleuron*, a
journal devoted to the typographic arts which Morison later edited (Oliver
Simon was editor at the time). Gill refused, saying "Typography is not my
line of country". A distinguished colleague of Morison, Beatrice Warde
admitted in a radio programme about Morison that as a potential type-
designer she regarded Gill as "a very unlikely one" when Morison was first
considering him.

This is not surprising when one thinks about the differences between
cutting letters directly into a surface and designing a metal type which a
printer can use in various sizes and for a variety of typographic purposes. It
is therefore worth mentioning some of these differences.

Roman capitals are the source of all the letterforms used in the Western
alphabet. Their design and proportions were arrived at in Roman times and
can be seen in many inscriptions as examples of grace, economy and fitness
to purpose. They are essentially inscriptional letters: even when the Romans
used them for less permanent writings than stone inscriptions they incised
them, probably in wax, with a point, or stylus. Paper (though already

invented) had not become available in Rome during the great period of classic inscriptional lettering, some of which survives.

The main distinguishing characteristic of roman letters is their serifs, and it is by these that we now classify "roman" as distinct from other types, called "sans-serif". The serif is probably a convention of the stonemason. It is neater, when incising lines with a chisel, to terminate the lines with a serif than to cut the acute angles which would be needed for the terminations of sans-serif letters. Roman capitals in print are, therefore, a survival, to some extent, of the stonemason's art, retaining their serifs though, in strict logic, these may be said no longer to fulfil their original purpose.

The inscriptional roman alphabet used only capital letters. The "minuscule" alphabet (the printer's "lower-case") was derived directly from the capitals and, later, scribes adapted the more geometrical forms to a cursive (or "running") script appropriate to the pen rather than the chisel. But even the lower-case letters, in both script and type, may retain something of the serif and we are forced to conclude that, whatever may have been the convenience of the serif to the letter cutter in stone, it acquired, in time, a positive value to the reader of print and made for legible and pleasing letterforms.

The lower-case roman alphabet has not the classical authority of the capitals. Though derived from the capitals there are, so far as I know, no inscriptional models of roman lower-case from Roman times. Every letter in the printer's lower-case is derived from its capital equivalent and is, strictly speaking, a distortion of the capital for informal use. The true cursives — the Italianate or "italic" hands of the writing masters — were essentially pen-formed letters and needed modifications of design and connecting strokes so that they could be written in a flowing way. Most of these modifications have been retained in today's informal lettering and the

*Lettering for Count Harry
Kessler's Insel Verlag*

MAX GOERTZ

ZWEI NOVELLEN

roman lower-case in printing has also conserved a vertical emphasis and spacing, and the serifs, characteristic of the capitals.

Lower-case roman, therefore, offers greater freedom to the letter-designer, a freedom which has been known to lead to licence. Gill's lower-case romans show great restraint and simplicity, and his incised italics maintain the historical distinctions between roman and italic – the former's feeling of dignity and the latter's sense of cursive movement and lightness.

Robert Harling took the view that "his attempts to design an italic were most successful when he followed Mr Stanley Morison's proposals concerning the virtues of the sloped roman" ("Eric Gill's Pilgrim Type", *Penrose Annual* 47, 1953) but an examination of the Gill italic types does not entirely bear this out. In *An Essay on Typography* Gill remarks "Most italic type faces . . . are too sloping and too cursive. There is a great need of a narrow and less sloping letter, which, while giving emphasis and difference, shall be of the same non-cursive character as the upright letters they are used with", which would seem to place him in accord with Morison on the subject of italic. Yet he does not stick to the roman form for lower-case italic types and, in Perpetua italic (named Felicity) the letters a and g are distinctly cursive in inspiration, while an earlier (unused) draft design for a Perpetua italic which Gill made in 1926 is even more distinctly of pen-formed origins, as is the lower-case g of his Joanna italic.

Gill always showed respect for classical models. After all, he had been a pupil of Edward Johnston who – at one time virtually single-handed – had resisted the further deterioration of the roman and italic alphabets into weak, badly conceived forms at the hands of signwriters and others: the success of Johnston, and those who followed his careful, respectful and altogether craftsmanlike approach to lettering, can be seen in today's standards in typography and signwriting which are overall very much superior to those of the early 1900s when Johnston started to revive classical models.

But it should be emphasized that, though Johnston and, later, Gill, worked from classical models they were not enslaved by them. Gill himself explained this in *An Essay on Typography* (p. 43) "Letters are letters. A is A and B is B. The lettermaker of the twentieth century has not got to be an inventor of letter forms but simply a man of intelligence and good will. . . . As the Roman, when he thought of lettering thought of inscription letters; as the medieval man thought of written letters; so in the twentieth century, when we write a letter carefully we call it 'printing'" and, later in the *Essay*, he drove the point further home by saying of inscriptions, ". . . while we may remember Trajan lovingly in the museum we must forget all about him in the workshop."

The essential quality of the incised letter is that it is three-dimensional: it has been cut either into, or out of, a hard surface, and no photograph can show this because a photograph is two-dimensional: perspective gives an illusion of depth. The point is relevant to a major difference between inscriptional lettering and type. Incised letters obtain their effect through a number of related circumstances – the colour and nature of the material, the depth of the incision, the direction from which the light falls, the size of the inscription, and so on. Type is assumed to exist for reading at normal distance and, of course, is strictly two-dimensional. Of vital importance in type is that its letters must be capable of being used in one of the mechanical systems used for text composition. It can easily be seen why Gill at first did not feel that there was an obvious correlation between being able to cut fine alphabets and design good types: both he and Morison knew better than that.

Another difference between letter-cutting and type design may be noted because it is important to the way in which Gill went about the task of type design. Letter-cutting has to be done directly, and the cutter cannot afford to make a mistake. On the other hand he has considerable freedom, within his chosen design, to arrange the inscription in a way which he judges best suited to its purpose. In doing so he may vary letter-spacing, line spacing and other formal elements as well as the design of individual letters. The letter forms of a printing type are of fixed sizes and are cast in metal so that spatial and other relationships are predetermined for a particular size within the mechanical parameters of the typesetting system and of a particular typeface. More importantly, from the type-designer's standpoint, letters for casting as printing type can be modified throughout the stages which precede the actual cutting of the punches from which the type will be produced.

Gill's transition from letter-cutter to type-designer was undoubtedly helped by three things: his love of experiment – of "trying things out", his readiness to do the meticulous work needed to make letters "work" in typographic terms, and his facility with the calligraphic and brush-based lettering techniques which a type-designer uses. Gill's inspiration was disciplined by a practical approach to the job, derived from the careful planning and drafting which precedes the execution of incised lettering. He did not, in short, need to learn the lessons of patient experiment, careful comparison, meticulous measurement and fine discrimination which go into the creation of a new type.

Gill was certainly prepared to adapt the letter-cutter's standards to the different task of type design, but he saw no reason to abandon altogether the freedom of the letter-cutter for a rigidly mechanistic approach. Indeed, Gill made some workmanlike adaptations of technique to allow him to use his writing tools for type design in a way to which he was accustomed and which was congenial to him.

The type-designer works his ideas out in letters drawn on a much larger scale than they will be when cast, though he must constantly bear in mind the ultimate need for reduction and the changes in scale which take place over the various point sizes. Small details on large letters can disappear when reduced, yet irregularities of form which are not conspicuous in the large draft will sometimes become mysteriously exaggerated in the smaller version. Again, the type-designer has to remember the mechanical nature of the printing process; for example delicately drawn serifs, fine lines and other small details which add to the character or delicacy of a drawn or incised letter may not be practical when, in type, they have to withstand the mechanical pressures of the letterpress printing machine, or be used to cast a stereo or a duplicate plate.

Gill knew this, of course. Several times he ingeniously overcame the problems of scale by deliberately drawing letters as small as was practicable (and

of generations it would last. The richest hoped it might last for ten. Our traditions say, in the second generation after Agamemnon the deluge came.

It came, the ancients said, in the form of the avenging Heraclids, come back to regain the heri-

ABCDEFGHIJKLMNOPQRSTUVWXYZ

Æ Œ Ç Qu

abcdefghijklmnopqrstuvwxyz

fi ff fl ffi ffl & ç

1234567890

. , ; : - ' ! ? ( ) " "

Proof of Malin's hand-cut punches from Gill's original design for Perpetua

this, for Gill, was really quite small: between 18 and 24 point in a few cases). He would then have these letters enlarged so that he could examine them with all their imperfections of detail. From such englargements he would draw further alphabets on a large scale, using his preliminary enlarged draft as a guide. Finally the perfected "second-stage" alphabet would be reduced, once more, to the small size. By such a procedure he was able to work with some confidence that his large-scale drafting was truly workable in the smaller sizes. Gill used this method in the preliminary stages of designing the Golden Cockerel type (see page 77).

There are grounds for believing that, despite his disclaiming any knowledge of type design before starting his collaboration with The Monotype Corporation in 1925, Gill had already used something like the above technique for modifying the letter forms of existing types, perhaps for his own practice and pleasure, or perhaps with a craftsman's curiosity about the techniques of an adjacent craft. An illustration to an article entitled "Eric Gill, Master of Letter Forms", by William B. Holman in *The Library Chronicle* of the University of Texas at Austin (New Series No 2, November 1970) is captioned; "Gill's earliest known type design to be reproduced, dated June 1914." This was fourteen years before he tackled Perpetua! There are resemblances to Perpetua and, for that matter, to Bembo. It is the opinion of John Dreyfus of The Monotype Corporation, with whom I agree on this, that the design was either based on, or actually "worked up" from designs which appeared in a type specimen book from the typefounder Miller & Richards.

Mr Dreyfus has also shown me a photocopy of a type design which he has seen in the Gill collection at the University of San Francisco. It is dated Ditchling Common, Sussex, 15th June 1914.

In the Monotype Gill collection there is a sheet with a few letters which suggests that Gill was, around 1932, toying with the idea of designing a revised version of Monotype Baskerville, but nothing more seems to have come of this. By this time Gill was under contract to The Monotype Corporation and, with his customary energy and passion for work, may well have undertaken such preliminary experiments from enthusiasm, or a desire to give "value for money" to the Corporation or even from the sheer delight of using his relatively newly-found technical equipment as a type designer.

In the same collection an unusual technique for creating the large original letters for a typeface design is seen in a version of Jubilee (see page 75) in which Gill has cut the letters out of a light, white board, as he would cut a stencil, and backed the cut-outs with a matt black paper. Here indeed – even with a letter which can be called "calligraphic" – do we see the immense precision and dexterity of a letter-*cutter* in action in two-dimensional letter design!

Gill never cut punches himself, and only one of his typefaces, Perpetua, was hand-cut by Charles Malin in Paris who, as a contributor to *The Monotype Recorder* (Vol 41, No 3, 1958) remarks "succeeded only too well in reproducing, on the tiny scale of type, the shapes and details of the stone cutter's model letters". It is intriguing to speculate on what the writer really meant by that rather frosty phrase "only too well"! To some who have a real knowledge of types and what they are used for, those first proofs of Perpetua – the "stone-cutter's letters" transformed into printed letters – may have seemed rather too chiselled and lapidiary.

Collections of Gill's preliminary design work in many parts of the world all testify to his patience and persistence in "getting things right" to the last detail before he was satisfied with a type design. Many alternative letter forms are tried out and designs are brought again and again to a high finish so that they can be judged and examined. In a few cases more than one version of a type has existed to trick the memories of typophiles and complicate the task of commentators. For example the first (1931) edition of *An Essay of Typography* shows Gill's Perpetua with a "sloped roman" italic as advocated by Stanley Morison (see page 38) but the 1936 edition of the *Essay* replaces this with the more cursive and calligraphic italic called Felicity, which is now the accepted italic for Perpetua.

Evidence of Gill's early interest in type design: his "improved 'old style' long primer" dated by Gill "15 June 1914" and probably drawn over a Miller & Richard's type specimen

TESTIMONIALS
THIS desirable looking apparatus is considered the best for the *purpose*.

MARY BEATRICE
only daughter
of Walter Consitt Boulter.
Vicar of this Parish. died 12 Mar.
1902. in her 21st. year.
She was a student of the
Royal Academy of Arts
& Organist of this Church.
This window. patterned on
one formerly existing here.
together with the glass showing what things she loved.
was dedicated
in memory of her.
24 Feb. 1906.

Gill's incised lettering for a
tablet (1906) shows
similarities to his later
work on roman types.
(Original size, $19\frac{1}{4} \times 30\frac{1}{2}$

There were long discussions between Gill and Morison ranging over many things other than type and Gill worked closely, also, with the technicians at the Monotype works and at the Monotype drawing office. This is not to imply that Gill meekly accepted every limitation and suggestion without question or argument. He was critical and demanding when confronted with technical reasons for modifying letters and more than once voiced his impatience with the "mechanical methods" by which types come into being. The machines he accepted, but was determined that they would serve, not master him. Nevertheless he grew to respect the specialized knowledge and skills he found within The Monotype Corporation: it was, perhaps for Gill, a salutary experience to collaborate with people who, though serving commercial ends within a factory, were sensitive and responsive to aesthetic qualities as well as being capable of a standard of workmanship which Gill could readily appreciate and admire. He expressed his admiration for them more than once. In his *Autobiography* he wrote of his type designing for The Monotype Corporation that "few associations can have been either more honourable or more pleasant – or, from my point of view, more helpful".

4

TYPE IN USE

THOUGH TYPOGRAPHERS AND SPECIALISTS TEND TO DISCUSS type in the abstract – to compare one type with another – it is obvious that a typeface is functioning properly only when it becomes part of the printed page and can be read. This is why the layman finds it difficult to assess the finer qualities of a type from specimen alphabets and why the professional typographer can also be misled without the guidance of specimen settings. The considerations in choosing a type are further complicated by: the influence of materials other than type (inks and papers); colours; the presence or absence of illustrations; the printing process used; and, of course, by the efficiency or otherwise of the designer in correlating these characteristics. Type is, therefore, only part of what is involved in designing for print and, important though it is, should not be detached from the elements which surround it. There are no "perfect" types in the sense that there are no all-purpose types and, while it is possible to assess whether a type has been used carelessly, there are no set rules by which a type can be displayed to its best advantage. All this leaves the question of what is appropriate in setting a type very much within the realm of habit, taste, judgement, fashion and other variables.

Fashion and availability are probably the most potent factors in deciding the survival of a display typeface, but it is the typographical conservatism of the book which has been the strongest preserving influence on the use of the classic typefaces. The differing needs of the advertising industry – mainly those of novelty and arresting design – have forced designers to search for "new" types for no better reason than their contrast with "old" or merely familiar types. Fashion may dictate that a type which is unpopular today will be in demand tomorrow for the same sort of reasons that fashion in dress tends always to look for something different from what is currently available, often finding it in a past fashion. The analogy between fashions in clothes and fashions in type can usefully be sustained, though it should not be taken too far.

In Gill's day the typographical scene was different from the present one, partly because the printing industry relied more on the letterpress process and on conventional hot-metal typesetting and partly because the communications media were less pervasive and less demanding of the designer than they are today. Then, as now, the appearance of a piece of printing was dependent on the combined skills of designer and printer, though the printer was also the designer more often than is now the case. The typographer's repertoire was smaller due to the absence of highly developed illustration reproduction methods, and also for a number of technical reasons inherent in the printing processes; customers were more easily satisfied with what they could get than the majority would now be. Greater variety and versatility in printing techniques have not always enhanced legibility nor invariably worked well for the reader. But, generally speaking, the jobbing printers of the 1920s and 30s were less responsive to the values and virtues of the typographical niceties than they now need to be to stay in business. They worked by rule of thumb and, often, the rule bore little relationship to the craft status to which they laid claim. Gill was irritated and impatient with an industrial system which he thought cramped and devalued the work of men's hands and minds and his criticism extended to printing, though he also saw the printer's opportunity to demonstrate how much could be done under factory conditions to improve the quality of what was made and to reassert the dignity and authority of the maker.

Designing new types may now seem to be a small contribution to the problems of making people aware of the printed page as a piece of fine craftsmanship or, more humbly, as an exercise in good industrial design. But, with the reservations already made, one can see that, without good types, the typographer or printer rarely works with pleasure and inspiration and, while originality is not always the key to success, it too is a means of finding ways of making type work harder and better in its various roles.

Gill may not have thought typographical originality very important. His view of the letter was, so to speak, from the inside. Not only did he know what letters were – how they were made and how they could be made to behave in different ways in different contexts – he also knew what many of the letters he saw in print lacked: what they were not and yet what they could be. Many of the types in common commercial use were not beautiful; not efficient. That is to say they embodied distortions, sometimes grotesque, of the classic roman proportions which had long been the ground-plan of fine lettering. ("Grotesque" was the name applied, at first derisively, to sansserif types by those who regarded the classic romans as the only decent tradition of letter design. It stuck, though "grots" are now quite respectable.)

D P D Q R W
S T U V X Y U
A B C D D D E F G J
H K L M N P R S T V
A E H K L M N
B F P R S T U J
I V W X Y X Z
O Q C G D D D
D E F G H K J
L M N O
I W X Y Z O Q Q
Eric G

In all this the lettering artist in stone, the calligrapher and, in a slightly different context, the private press printer, could go their own ways so long as they could obtain work of the sort they could do best. The lettering artist and letter-cutter, such as Gill was in 1924 when he and Morison first met, could afford to be selective and critical since they were truly "creators of letters". The first drafts which Gill did for Perpetua were uncompromisingly the kind of letters he might have designed for cutting, not for typefounding.

James Moran says that "After being converted to the idea that his lettering could be transformed into type he [Gill] suddenly became a typographical authority." (*Stanley Morison, his typographical achievement*; Lund Humphries, 1971). The judgement is rather harsh and does not distinguish between Gill the typographer and Gill the type designer. Long before he started to design types Gill had cultivated an appreciation of the printed page as an illustrator. He was sensitive to the nuances of good typography and made what seems a perfectly rational distinction between *using* type and *designing* type. As to the former, Gill could hardly have been unaware of much of what Morison told him about the general disposition and appearance of type on a page, or have disagreed fundamentally with the typographical standards which Morison was advocating. And, as has now been discovered, Gill was interested enough in type to have drawn alphabets for type as early as 1917.

It is surprising that, when Gill became, for the first time, a printer in his own right it was not as a private press printer but as the proprietor of a commercial printing house, with his son-in-law René Hague. As Hague & Gill this was started in 1933 and by this time Gill's robust rejection of all that was not the product of the craftsman's mind and hands had softened and modified. He was ready to join battle for sound printing at a stage when real progress was being made and at a point where his experience and talents could find an outlet. It would be possible to call Gill an opportunist, but the writer believes it more accurate, as well as more charitable, to see him as an enthusiast whose enthusiasms were consuming and powerful. At any event he specifically rejected the notion that his was a private press. "It would be strictly correct to say we have started a printing business," he said in a letter in the *Monotype Recorder*, Autumn 1933. Gill went on to say, "It is, of course, difficult to define the term 'private press', but it seems clear to me that the real distinction between such a press and others is not in the typographical quality of the work it does or in the typographical enthusiasm of its proprietors, but simply in the fact that a 'private' press prints solely what it chooses to print, whereas a 'public' press prints what its customers demand of it."

Initial letters cut in wood for the Cranach Press

Gill never devoted himself for any lengthy period solely to the craft of arrangement and design in type and illustration. He worked in practical ways on projects that interested him and usually preferred the fluidity of a "free" design – engraved letters, devices and illustrations – without the constricting demands of everyday commercial work. Yet it is (with some reservations)

CANTICUM CANTICORUM

Jam enim hiems transiit;
imber abiit, et recessit.
Flores apparuerunt in terra nostra,
tempus putationis advenit;
vox turturis audita est in terra nostra;
ficus protulit grossos suos;
vineae florentes
dederunt odorem suum.
Surge, amica mea, speciosa mea,
et veni:
columba mea, in foraminibus petrae,
in caverna maceriae,
ostende mihi faciem tuam.
Sonet vox tua in auribus meis;
vox enim ua dulcis,
et facies tua decora.
Capite nobis vulpes parvulas
quae demoliuntur vineas;
nam vinea nostra floruit.
Dilectus meus mihi, et ego illi,
qui pascitur inter lilia,
donec aspiret dies,
et inclinentur umbrae.
Revertere; similis esto, dilecte mi,
capreae,
hinnuloque cervorum
super montes Bether.

10

QUOD EST SALOMONIS

SPONSA

IN lectulo meo, per noctes,
quaesivi quem diligit
anima mea;
quaesivi illum, et non inveni.
Surgam, et circuibo civitatem;
per vicos et plateas
quaeram quem diligit anima mea;
quaesivi illum, et non inveni.
Invenerunt me vigiles
qui custodiunt civitatem:
Num quem diligit anima mea vidistis?

11

Page from "the Song of Songs" with wood engraving and initial letter by Gill for the Cranach Press of Count Harry Kessler (1931)

easier to design a text or title page for a fine limited edition – a page containing specially created devices and illustrations and printed on fine paper – than to apply oneself to such everyday things as the design of official forms, newspaper pages and the like. The typographer who works out a good typographical solution to the presentation of a railway timetable may convincingly argue that he is doing something more difficult than the "artist" typographer with a long tradition of bookwork on which to draw for inspiration and emulation. He is really doing something entirely different: in typography the final result is all-important.

Be this as it may, Gill's distinction between industrial typography (which we might now call commercial typography) and "humane typography" would be neither helpful nor easily understood today. In his *Essay on Typography* (which I will deal with in greater detail in a later chapter) there is an uneasy impression that Gill never clearly declared what he thought typography was for. Further, though Gill no doubt believed that he was breaking new ground and raising new standards, much of the essay reflects what could be described as an old-fashioned view of the craft of typographical design and, in places, a sentimental one, blurred by Gill's mystical belief in the "holiness" of some work contrasted with the "profanity" of the rest.

Gill was being deliberately naïve, or at least over-simplifying the typographer's task, when he argued that "elegant poetry should have elegant type, and the rough-hacked style of Walt Whitman a rough hacked style of letter; the reprints of Malory should be printed in 'blackletter' and books of technology in 'sans-serif'". Such guidance, so far as it goes, helps people to realize that type on the page is intrinsic with the page and the import of the words, but if followed would result in typographic infelicities which would be hard to tolerate today. Gill, it seems, did not feel that a technical book needed to be as *legible* as a poem. While the same typefaces may not be appropriate to both, the basic consideration of the typographer is not clever analogy – "sans" for technique and blackletter for antique – but legibility, above all; type is for readers, not for typographers.

Of more immediate interest and importance is the use which has been made of the types which Gill helped to create. Gill Sans has always been a popular type face and this is due to much more than its originality at the time it was first made available. Besides the intrinsic quality of the face, it has been cut in so wide a range of weights and sizes that it can – and occasionally has – been used for everything from newspaper headlines to fine book printing. Fashion, as usual, has had something to do with it but it was the typographical design, not the typeface itself, which so upset the worthy Master

Printers when it was flaunted before them at the British Federation of Master
Printers' Annual Congress at Blackpool in 1928. Morison (who designed the
programme) and Gill may both, in their different ways, have tried to appear
iconoclastic and may have enjoyed the *enfant terrible* image occasionally when
it seemed that people were not taking as much notice as they should of what
they were saying. But the visual characteristics of all Gill's types (with the
possible exception of Gill Ultra Bold and the unfortunate Jubilee) are sober,
pure and far removed from any eccentricity of form or intent. It has remained
for typographers with a different set of preoccupations and priorities than
either Morison or Gill had in their time to show how versatile they are.

5

THE ESSAY ON
TYPOGRAPHY

GILL WROTE, TALKED AND ARGUED ABOUT ALL THE THINGS he considered important. He was eager to share his views and did so in lectures, correspondence, essays and journalism. It is easy now for less generous-minded people than Gill to find contradictions and occasional absurdities in what he wrote. The *Essay on Typography* (first published by Sheed and Ward in 1931), which is of particular interest in our present context, would probably not serve as a textbook for a typographic design student today and it may seem odd that a man who, in 1924 was artlessly disclaiming any knowledge of the subject, could, seven years later, write a textbook on typography; for this was clearly what Gill intended his *Essay* to be. It contains a good deal of theoretical discussion and practical advice, including a chapter on punch-cutting which shows how intrigued Gill had been, after his association with The Monotype Corporation, in mechanical methods for making type. Some of the *Essay* is as valid now as it was more than forty years ago, mainly where Gill's concern with fundamental principles are not subject to the changes of fashion. But the *Essay* does not now enjoy a very wide readership, not least because so many of the lessons which Gill was trying to teach have been put into practice by typographers and designers.

It is superfluous to quote extensively from the *Essay*: it is there for anyone to read. I am devoting a chapter to it more for its indirect illumination of Gill's personality and ideas than for any immediate insight it gives into his methods of type design. The *Essay* can profitably be examined, now, from the standpoint of the changes which have taken place since it was written. In the 30s there were many battles still to be fought against the drab commercialism which was overtaking so much printing at the time. The jobbing printers of the day were losing sight of traditions which were more than mere craft survivals from an earlier and less mechanized era of typography. Gill had caught the flavour of such crusading from Edward Johnston and was ready to broaden the front.

Some of the aggressiveness which occasionally shows through in the writing of the *Essay* may conceal a certain ambivalence in Gill's attitude to a world from which he was still somewhat removed in spirit and temperament. In the first pages of the *Essay* Gill is already harping on the dichotomy between crude industrialism and hand craftsmanship. In the typographical field – then as now – such simple distinctions were not always so profitable. Whether type is composed by hand or machine, or impressions made by hand-press or power-press, there is little comparison between the techniques and tools of the printer and those of the true hand craftsman. Furthermore it does not follow that a "craft" approach to print will necessarily produce a higher-grade work than a "commercial" one. Gill recognized this in his own way when he wrote that it was worth discovering "what kind of things can be made under a system of manufacture which, whatever its ethical sanction or lack of sanction, is certainly the system we have, the system of which we are proud and the system few desire to alter".

But he was never really happy with "the system" and, even after he had himself shown that machinery could be responsive to the dictates of the creative imagination, he chafed; as when he wrote, of his Joanna type, that it was "not designed to facilitate punch-cutting. Not at all. Machines can do practically anything. The question isn't what they *can* but what they *should*." If Gill could not always sound convincing about the need for people to do things with their own hands he might, so to speak, persuade the machines to do his bidding – make them work well for him and for the others who used their products.

Private presses certainly operate "on human lines", but there are commercial printers who practise sound workmanship and felicitous design who now find parts of the *Essay* rather irritating: for example when Gill asserts blandly that handmade papers are "the best" without reference to the typographical considerations involved in choosing papers. The hand-press printer was urged to make his own ink because this required patience and "To be patient is to suffer". Today we may feel that there is enough suffering in good printing without adding to it!

The printer had other mentors – Morison, Oliver Simon and Beatrice Warde among them – who did as much, and more, than Gill to remind him of what was important, and in danger of being mislaid in the scramble to meet the rapidly expanding demand for print. But, unlike Gill, such reformers did not insist that the battle be joined between hand craftsmanship and industrial production but rather between that which was sound and appropriate to the job and that which was careless, inefficient and wasteful.

Gill, as I have already said, did not readily acknowledge how much could be achieved by the intelligent use of machinery. At best he thought it a mixed blessing, even when used well. "It is abundantly clear," he wrote in the *Essay*, "that while the apparent powers of the machine punch-cutting process are unlimited, its actual powers are limited to the production of only the most simple and demonstrably measurable kinds of letters. There is, however, a large field for the simple and measurable, and it will soon be clear, even to the owners of punch-cutting machinery, still more to book publishers and designers of letters, that, as in architecture, furniture-making and the making of all mechanically manufactured articles, an absolute simplicity is the only legitimate, because the only respectable, quality to be looked for in the products of industrialism." This, when the types of Caslon, Fournier and Baskerville had been cut by machinery, was selling machines a little short!

Agreed, there was little evidence around in Gill's time of a willingness on the part of the manufacturers to look as lovingly and carefully at the functional efficiency of their products as he would have wished, though he was wrong in asserting that the world of mechanized industry and those who chose "to be masters of their own work in their own workshops" were two worlds which would never become "one flesh". If anybody was a master of his own work it was Gill himself and, for him, the punch-cutting machinery and its operators had succeeded in making available typefaces which set new standards of elegance, subtlety and usefulness. Neither Perpetua nor Joanna are, in the narrow sense, "simple and measurable" faces and Gill Sans was, perhaps, less "simple and measurable" after the punch-cutters had done their work than when Gill first drafted it.

Reading the *Essay* today one must keep in mind that Gill was engaged on a "cleaning-up" operation. For example, he discusses "poster letters" which we would now loosely categorize as "display types". At present typographers have at their disposal an extremely wide variety of display types, many of them arresting and some of them pleasing. But Gill saw only that "The business of poster letters . . . has not been extricated from the degradations imposed on it by an insubordinate commercialism" and, at the time of writing this, he was right. Fashion may nowadays have gone too far in the use of out-of-the-ordinary, or frankly bizarre, letter-forms to arrest attention, but at least this can be counted better than the confused shouting of letters which, to make themselves heard, just got larger, blacker and heavier. So Gill

abcdefghijklmnopqrstuvwxy&z

abcdefghijklmnopqrstuvwxyz

abcdefghijklmnopqrstuvwxy&z

ΑΒΓΔΕΖΗΘΙΚΛΜΝΞΟΠΡΣΤΥΦΧΨΩ

αβγδεζηθικλμνξοπρστυφχψω

ΑΒΓΔΕΖΗΘΙΚΛΜΝΞΟΠΡΣΤΥΦΧΨΩ

αβγδεζηθικλμνξοπρστυφχψω

(Fig. 11: 1 & 2, Perpetua Roman capitals & lower-case; 3, Caslon Old Face Italic; 4, Perpetua Italic; 5 & 6, Porson Greek capitals and lower-case; 7 & 8, Perpetua Greek capitals & lower-case.)

by what the Emperor Peter the Great did in the case of Russian writing. The Russian alphabet is closely related to the Greek. The formalization of Russian script was achieved very successfully by the Dutch typographers employed by Peter the Great; and the same thing could be done for Greek. ¶ Many varieties of Greek types exist, but for the most part they are more italic than the Italics. In recent years attempts have been made at improvement, but no attempt has been made to take advantage of the fact that Greek capitals have always been made in

This page from the first edition of the Essay on Typography shows a "sloped roman" italic with Perpetua which, in later modifications, became Felicity italic, the italic normally used with this face

62 these are only partial survivals, & very few people could, without reference to ancient books, write down even a complete alphabet of either. As far as

a e f g
a e f g

(Figure 23: the upper line of letters is essentially 'Roman Lower-case'; the lower essentially 'Italic'.)

we are concerned in modern England, Roman Capitals, Lower-case and Italics are three different alphabets, and all are current 'coin'. But however familiar we are with them, their essential differences are not always easily discovered. It is not a matter of slope or of serifs or of thickness or thin-

Gill varied his italics between "sloped roman" and the more calligraphic form shown, particularly, in the letter g in this page from his Essay on Typography

attacked the problem as he saw it, re-establishing, in his *Essay*, criteria by which
work could be judged.

In many ways the Victorians had driven a wedge, not so much between
hand-made and machine-made things as between the concepts of utility
and "art". For Gill an "artist" was not a mere decorator of things for those
who could afford decoration but "one who makes his craft a fine art" (shorter
OED). The *Essay* struggles to remove the misplaced barriers between what
could be called beautiful, appropriate, enjoyable and "artistic" and what was
useful. To do so it was necessary to insist on "the plainest of plain things", if
only because plain things provided a better starting point for making the
best, rather than the worst, of more imaginative and decorative things. "The
only thing to do" Gill says, "is to make ourselves into such thoroughly and
completely rational beings that our instinctive and intuitive reactions and
responses and sympathies are more or less bound to be rational also", which
was rather like saying that if everybody were rational there would be no crime!

In the typographical sphere such a severe dictum is hard to apply, for type
does not possess this intrinsic "rationality" as a general attribute. The
typographer is not so much an arbiter of taste as one guided by necessity,
yet one who must retain and use what he believes to be tasteful.

The mainstream of typography, as Gill observed, runs through the printed
book where it preserves and perpetuates that which is worthy of preservation
and perpetuation, and where time has tested its adequacy to the reader's
needs. A look at the typography of the *Essay* itself is a practical demonstration
of Gill's view of book design. In the resetting of the *Essay* in 1954 Gill's
directives were followed as closely as in the original edition. We can see the
equal letter-spacing, the use of the "paragraph" sign in place of paragraph
indentation, and other typographical factors which Gill felt were necessary to
the text page. The main difference between the setting of the *Essay* and of
most other books is the unjustified right-hand margin. In the *Essay* Gill
argues for the validity of this way of setting text pages as opposed to the more
conventional way of setting text so that it lies "square" on the page with even
left- and right-hand margins. Legibility, Gill insists, is helped by even word-
spacing and, he says, it is absurd to sacrifice this advantage to gain right-hand
justification.

It can be mentioned, for those who do not know what is involved in
justifying type, that the method used is that of putting additional word spacing into a line to bring it out to the required measure. Where this is undesir-
able, owing to the excessive space between words which would occur in some
lines, word-break procedures are used which allow the compositor to carry

words over from one line to the next and retain reasonable word-spacing consistent with easy reading. It is argued, by Gill and others, that word-spacing is paramount in maintaining an easy-to-read text and justification of the right-hand margin is a convention which, since it prevents this, should go to the wall in text composition. Today we can find many examples of unjustified text setting, especially for short texts such as are found in advertising copy, though the book designer has, on the whole, retained his preference for a "square" page. Needless to say Gill did not give much weight to whatever preferences authors, publishers and public may have had in this matter!

The pros and cons may be discussed at a typographical level, but the real answer could come to something much more fundamental: we like what we know. In *The Anatomy of Judgement* by M. L. Johnson Abercrombie (Penguin) the author makes the point more elaborately. He says that any new object presented to the senses "must be soluble in old experience" and that people have a tendency "to ignore or reject that which does not fit in with the pattern". "The pattern", in the case of text setting, has long been established; even the scribes liked to use devices which expanded their line to bring it out for an even right-hand margin. The matter has never been settled satisfactorily. Among the arguments for justification the most convincing, to me, is the one which suggests that, when reading a continuous text, the brain, so-to-speak, "measures" the distance between the end of one line and the beginning of the next, and this allows the eyes to return without effort, and accurately, to the correct spot on the page for each line. When the lines are of slightly different length, as they are when text is set unjustified, the inequalities in lateral shift from right to left for each line is a source of optical fatigue.

In recent years the justified/unjustified controversy has been given a new twist – one which would probably have baffled Gill, or made him angry. The argument has passed from the typographical sector into the most automated and machine-dominated one of computer typesetting. Computers are used to implant certain typographical and format requirements into keyboarded text which were previously under the control of compositors but which, in the newer systems, are catered for by the computer programs. The computer's output, in this case, is a punched or magnetic tape which is used to drive the typesetting machine, which may be either a conventional "hot metal" machine or a photosetter. Most typographical needs, for example changes in size of type, capital letters, indentations and the like, can easily be programmed, but accurate and intelligent word-breaking in justified setting long proved difficult to program.

Word-breaks are carried out by compositors to a system which requires human judgement, and the reader's comprehension can be impaired by bad word-breaking. The *Rules for Compositors and Readers at the University Press, Oxford*, now in its 37th revised edition, states: "Avoid divisions if at all possible, having regard to the requirements of typography (even spacing, etc). Not to inconvenience the reader must always be one of the main considerations." Compositors are advised to divide words according to their etymology (e.g. atmo-sphere, bio-graphy) or, where such etymology is not immediately apparent, according to pronunciation (ab-stract, mini-ster). There are other rules to avoid: comic word breaks such as leg-end for "legend" and read-just for "readjust".

The point here is that word-break decisions are made by human intelligence and a knowledge of *how* people read as well as what they read. In recent times computer typesetting programming has largely overcome this problem, though at some effort and expense; only because, it would seem, so few were prepared to accept the easier solution of unjustified text, which would have been simpler for a computer to handle.

This digression is intended to draw attention to the power of convention in book typography – a power with which Gill did not fully reckon. In typography he was not dealing with the makeshift solutions of an upstart industry, but with an industry which had succeeded, to a remarkable extent, in using machinery to a variety of ends. There is (and how Gill would have hated being told so) a touch of the amateur about some parts of the *Essay*, though there is no doubt at all that Gill's heart was in the right place. He argues in favour of the printed result given by the hand-press and says that the power-press needs a minder "to ensure that it runs regularly": the power-press printer does not have to consider "the trifling inconsistencies which are inseparable from any hand-operated tool" and obtains "a dead level of uniformity in which there is not the smallest apparent variation". None of this was true then, nor is it true now. Indeed, since the expansion of offset-lithography as one of the main printing processes it is even less likely that a machine-minder can let the press do all the work and still get a "dead level of uniformity"!

6

THE TYPES

PERPETUA

ERPETUA WAS THE FIRST TYPE DESIGNED BY GILL FOR THE Monotype Corporation and, many would say, the best. It is a true roman which also meets the needs of a printing type for use with modern printing processes without any loss of clarity and elegance. Around 1925, when Gill was engaged in designing Perpetua, there was considerable typographic interest in the revival of the classic roman letter-forms. The revival was not merely antiquarian in spirit; the roman letter was, as it has remained, the model for all typefaces of European descent, though its intrinsic beauty was often marred in printing types. There remained a few good book faces on classical lines but, with increasing mechanization and the use of a wide variety of papers, it was no longer as easy as it once was to match a type with the process and materials used for the range of work undertaken. Gill would certainly have agreed with those who were calling for better book types. His own inscriptional lettering was no slavish imitation of early models and he would have had no difficulty in sensing the enthusiasm of those who wanted a "modern" roman.

A set of roman capitals with lower case italic and figures copied from an instruction chart by Gill for Edward Johnston show the nature of the small, but important changes which he felt appropriate to contemporary taste and needs. Taking (as it is often taken) the Trajan column inscription as an ideal of roman letterform proportions, the difference between thick and thin strokes is more marked in the Gill version, the relationship of stroke thickness to letter height being in the order of 1:8 instead of the 1:10 of the Trajan lettering. The letters E, F and L are wider than Trajan, so is X, and the M narrower. The lower-case letters (not, of course, found in the Trajan inscription) are completely harmonious with the capitals, a remarkable achievement of extrapolation. But this alphabet was intended as a model for inscriptional lettering and there are features which would be unsuited to type, for example the delicacy of the serifs and the hairlines in some of the italic letters, both of which would easily be broken down under the mechanical stresses of letterpress printing.

It was the planning of Perpetua which brought Gill and Morison together as working partners for the first time. Morison is described by Ellic Howe as "a pioneer industrial designer" (which could hardly be said about Gill) and he would therefore have had clear ideas about what sort of design would suit both the market and the limitations of mechanical typesetting methods in common use. But he wanted Gill to design the typeface and knew that, to get him to do so, he would have to let Gill have his own way wherever possible. The result is demonstrably a success, and Perpetua combines the grace and presence of inscriptional roman with the robust appearance which is needed to give a type "colour" on the book page. Many of the classic book faces look altogether too light on the pages of modern books with their extremely smooth, white papers. Equally, books with half-tone illustrations or woodcuts need a well-coloured type to maintain a balance of weight between text and illustration. William Morris, for his books from the Kelmscott Press, had gone back further in history to solve this problem and revived textura (or "blackletter") which, though it has the needful weight, is not particularly suited to smooth papers nor is it very restful or legible in continuous text for today's readers.

The choice of a sculptor and letter-cutter as a designer for a new typeface must have seemed odd to some of Morison's associates, but they did not

---

12-Pt. Gill

HHAAHBBHCCHÇÇHDDHEEHFFHGGHIIHJJHKKHLLHMMHNNH
HOOHPPHQQHQuQuHRRHSSHTTHUUHVVHWWHXXHYYHZZH
HÆÆHŒŒH&c.,&c.   HHOOH.   May, 1928

mmaambbmccmççmddmeemffmggnhhniihjjhkkhllhoohpphqqh
krrksskttkuukvvkwwkxxkyykzzkææk œœk&c.,&c.
kfifikffffuflflkffiffikfflfflk

k,,k..k;;k::k!!k??k"'k""k""k--k((k

0011022033044055066077088099o
0319284075491306237861 7o

Perpetua 12 point caps, lower case and figures

know Gill as well as Morison did, nor, perhaps, had they seen so much of his work. The model alphabets for Perpetua were drawn in 1925. Thereafter a great deal of work was put in by Gill, Morison and others at The Monotype Corporation making the changes which would enable a printing type to be used in mechanical typesetting, yet still retain the attributes which Gill had given it.

The punches were cut by hand in Paris by Charles Malin, one of the last few craftsmen capable of this exacting craft. At a Symposium on the life and work of Eric Gill held at the Clark Library on 22 April 1967 and published by Dawson's Bookshop, Los Angeles, in 1968, Beatrice Warde said of the punch-cutting that, "It was Morison who made the bold and most unusual decision to postpone the moment of setting all those modern [punch-cutting] processes in train until the design . . . had been cut by hand – that is by the exquisitely skilful use of file and graver on little blanks of soft steel, which was for centuries the normal and only way of relief-cutting the master letters, called punches, of which printing types are the mechanical replicas. Old Charles Malin of Paris was at that time one of the few surviving practitioners of that arduous craft. To him Morison took Gill's alphabet drawings . . . Malin's version, cut under a magnifying glass in letters about a sixth of an inch high, unconsciously demonstrated how much more than superlative skill of hand is needed to produce a fine typeface. Malin had followed his models with what we call "slavish" fidelity. Details which would have gone sweetly into the light and shadow of a large stone-incised alphabet became obtrusive in twelve point type." In this Mrs Warde seems to be having reservations about the success with which Gill's original drawings for Perpetua had been adapted to the visual characteristics of a printing type. Anyway, it was the first and only Monotype face which was hand-cut. "If the new Perpetua was to be as book-worthy as the roman that Martin had cut for John Bell, it might as well have its trial cutting by the same technique," commented a contributor to *The Monotype Recorder* (Vol 41, No 3, 1958). (Mr John Dreyfus has kindly pointed out an error in this last quotation: it was Richard Austin and not Martin who cut the Bell type.)

Malin's punches were struck and fitted by a French foundry, Ribadeau Dumas, and Gill quickly learned, from seeing the work smoke-proofed, what amendments were needed to make a good printing type and, one feels, may have developed a similar respect for the technicalities of typefounding to that which he undoubtedly had for good type on the page. At first he was prepared to go ahead with little obvious attention to technicalities; at least he seemed always ready to dismiss them impatiently, or to leave them to others.

He acknowledged the contribution made by the punch-cutter, however, in an article for *The Fleuron* (No 7, 1929) in which he says that his drawings for Perpetua "were not made with special reference to typography — they were simply letters drawn with brush and ink", but adds, "For the typographical quality of the fount and also for the remarkably fine and precise cutting of the punches, The Monotype Corporation is to be praised". Of the typeface he says, "In my opinion Perpetua is commendable in that, in spite of many distinctive characters, it retains that commonplaceness and normality which is essential to all good book-type".

Gill was right. Too much can be made of the differences between drawn and engraved letters; these are important, but they do not override the need for a consistently executed ground plan for the alphabets. Only a designer who knows exactly what he is trying to achieve can implant into a type design the harmonious and concordant qualities which a type such as Perpetua possesses.

The first specimens of Perpetua were shown in a translation of *The Passion of Saints Perpetua and Felicity* in 1928 and, in the same year, Gill started work on a series of sans-serif caps, lower case and italic which was to become Gill Sans. Perpetua was more of a novelty in its time than may now be realized. It was the first classic roman typeface to be designed specifically for machine composition and it has stood the test of time — a test which is probably as severe for a typeface as it is for any manufactured thing. Subsequent revivals

LMNQ
YZÆŒ

Gill's early draft for Perpetua, showing ligatures

ABCDEFG
HIJKLMN
QPQRSTU
VWXYZ2
&1234567
890£.,:;!?-

123 45687

Early Gill drawings for
Perpetua bold and
figures, dated 1933

of roman text faces have provided the book printer with a fine typographical repertoire.

Today's emphasis on the offset lithographic process of printing for books may have contributed to the printer's preference for types less small on the body than Perpetua, but it has held its own and Perpetua Titling is often seen where its authoritative and aristocratic tone is called for. In *Methods of Book Design* (2nd Edition, Faber, 1966) Hugh Williamson comments; "Gill's originality appears most clearly in the roman lower-case, in which several letter-forms are new in detail; all are adapted from alphabets designed for engraving in stone or wood. The capitals are conspicuously shorter than the ascenders, another characteristic of early old faces. The lower-case is rather 'modern' in appearance, having thin hair-lines and strong main strokes; the top serifs, in the smaller founts, are unbracketed hair-lines, but they are not quite horizontal, nor is the stress quite vertical."

The *Encyclopaedia of Typefaces* by Berry, Johnson and Jaspert (4th edition, Blandford, 1971) shows both Monotype Perpetua and a foundry type, Stephenson Blake Perpetua, the latter displaying some slight differences in design from the former. The italic designed by Gill for use with Perpetua is called Felicity, and a bold italic was added to the range after Gill's death by Monotype, though Gill showed a "sloped roman" italic with the Perpetua specimen in the first edition of his *Essay on Typography*.

Felicity is somewhat more conventional than Joanna italic (see page 38) and has its own italic caps. The inclination is slight and the figures are particularly attractive. There is, as Mr Williamson observed, an old face "feel" about Perpetua, though it does not have the weight of serif which characterizes most old-face types in which the shading has a vertical stress.

Robert Harling, in his article on Eric Gill's type designs, says that Perpetua was a prototype towards which Gill had been working steadily, and that it influenced not only Gill's later designs but also those of other designers. He notes that "apart from Jubilee, none of Gill's later type designs departed radically from the essential structure of the letter forms in Perpetua upper and lower-case". Harling concludes that "these freer forms were the result of a break from many years of primary preoccupation with the chiselled roman form", which is true, though Gill's dexterity is evident in the translation of chiselled forms into two-dimensional letterforms on the page. When *The Times* changed its text face to Morison's Times New Roman in 1932 the Perpetua capitals were retained for the main heading of the picture page where they had been since December 1929 because, wrote Morison in a *Times* article, "They could not be surpassed."

It may also be noted that in Perpetua, and later typefaces, as well as in his inscriptional lettering, Gill had completed a journey away from the essentially pen-formed letters which were the forte of his teacher, Edward Johnston; and, in virtually everything of value designed by Gill in his maturity, the forms are roman: even Gill Sans is appreciably more roman in feeling, in spite of its lack of serifs, than Johnston's Underground letter (q, n. page 54).

PERPETUA GREEK

GREEK TYPEFACES HAVE A HISTORY OF THEIR OWN. THEY were more widely used in print before the printer accepted the more diverse tasks which became his in the wake of increasing literacy, taking him away from the narrower rôle of publisher of scholarly texts. Greek types were first used in 1465 from punches cut by Peter Schoeffer, though this was a crude type which used some roman letters mixed in with the Greek ones.

Aldus Manutius's Greek face of 1496 was an early and fine example of a text face which had considerable influence on later designs. Jenson designed a fine Greek face in 1471. The general tendency was to prefer an italic style letter for Greek, but Gill's Perpetua Greek is uncompromisingly roman in inspiration and modelling. Among Gill's rough notes which accompany a draft for Perpetua Greek he makes direct comparisons between the Greek letters and their roman derivatives, the more to emphasize his intention of keeping as many of the roman characteristics as possible intact in the Greek, e.g.: "Γ = F without the middle bar. Δ = A without crossbar & with bottom of stems closed? Θ = O with middle bar added" and so on throughout the upper and lower case alphabet.

Of the modern Greek typefaces then available, Gill may have been unimpressed by what he saw. The Macmillan Greek of 1894 was heavy and

Part of a pasted-up specimen in which Gill has shown, by comparison with Perpetua roman, the essential similarity of design he was aiming for in Perpetua Greek

mannered and Proctor's Greek, though it had authority and dignity, was archaic in form. Gill gives 1929 in his *Autobiography* as the year in which Perpetua Greek appeared.

In the *Essay on Typography* Gill expressed what might be considered a predictable preference by an inscriptional craftsman for the roman-based forms of Greek when he wrote "Many varieties of Greek types exist, but for the most part they are more italic than the Italics. In recent years attempts have been made at improvement, but no attempt has been made to take advantage of the fact that Greek capitals have always been made in the same way as Roman capitals . . . The Perpetua Greek is the first example of an attempt to do for Greek what Peter the Great did for Russian and Jenson and others did for Latin".

With its strong family resemblance to roman, Perpetua Greek achieves its aim of providing a printing type in place of the calligraphically-rooted Greek types which were in common use and which, especially when mixed with roman text, looked wayward and odd. Beatrice Warde observed Gill's success with Perpetua Greek by noting that "a line of Greek enters the eye without giving the notion of a departure from the fount as matter-of-factly as would a quotation in Latin". A "modern" Greek typeface was welcomed for just such reasons. It was more than just an experiment, it stood in equable relationship to the roman type from which it was derived and, as does Perpetua roman, reveals the lightness and lack of self-consciousness which are the hallmarks of a Gill typeform.

Oddly enough, Perpetua Greek is not often encountered, and, in scholastic circles, there is an unaccountable preference for the less pleasing italic styles – evidence, perhaps, of the typographical truism that people "like what they know" and do not invariably appreciate the rationalizations and improvements which typographical logic dictates.

Among Gill's "experiments" are drawings of Hebrew and Arabic typefaces and he seems also to have contemplated a Greek face within the Joanna family, a few drafts of which exist in the Monotype House collection, though there is no evidence that it was ever cut and proofed.

GILL SANS

GILL SANS IS UNDOUBTEDLY GILL'S BEST-KNOWN TYPE AND probably one of the most successful sans-serif typefaces ever produced. When it was being cut there was already something of a rush to fill a need for new sans-serif types, and German typefounders were producing types of a "mechanical" character which reflected the anti-sentimental mood of the moderns inspired, according to Stanley Morison, by Edward Johnston's sans. Machines had become so respectable that it was thought desirable not to compromise with the fact that a thing was machine-made, rather to glory in it. Today, looking back on the design solutions of the post 1914–18 war period, we may feel that some were unnecessarily stark and simplified, though they stand in contrast to the self-conscious "prettiness" of much industrial design, including types, which had been admired by an earlier age. In this, typography, as it so often does, reflected the spirit of the time. There remained sound reasons for tempering experiment with some regard for tradition. After the cleansing and refreshing changes had gained momentum there was some quick back-tracking to recover the more durable virtues of the past which had been shed with the less attractive excesses of post-Victorian England. The printed book was, after all, already an extremely good piece of industrial design in its traditional form, which demanded roman type for its text. Only recently has sans-serif made a new bid for popularity as a text type, with qualified success.

But the 'thirties was also a period in which the quantity and variety of print was expanding, and new demands were therefore being made in many fields other than books. Educational and social changes were stimulating the need for print by more and more of the world's population; newspaper readership was rising, the newspapers themselves were changing in appearance to attract mass readership, popular magazines were being started and advertising becoming more adventurous in the new media. Together with this expansion of products, the printing industry's machinery, equipment and materials were being improved and some of the changes (principally higher production speeds and the wider variety of papers) had direct effects on the suitability or otherwise of the typefaces used.

The 1920s saw also the establishment of the jobbing printer in the urban scene. Until then the small one-man press was more likely to be a private printer than a commercial undertaking. Commercial jobbing houses, on the other hand, were less likely to pay attention to fine points of typography; they were little factories which met a local need as tradesmen and tried to do so as cheaply as possible. From the practical standpoint, therefore, and irrespective of any reasons advanced by designers, types which were clean and clear, which would stand up to mechanical strain, which could be used easily and without risk of clumsiness spoiling their effect, which would not

JOHNSTON

This broadsheet is set in Johnston type. Edward Johnston (1872-1944) was one of the followers of William Morris (1834-1896) who took a leading part in reviving an interest in good lettering after the decadence of the late-Victorian fashions. In 1916 Johnston was commissioned by Frank Pick (1878-1941) to design a special fount for the exclusive use of London's Underground and its associated companies. The resulting Johnston sans-serif type was the fore-runner of many sans-serif founts both in England and abroad, including that of Eric Gill (1882-1940) who was Johnston's friend and pupil in this specialised field of design. Johnston is the standard type used for all official signs and notices throughout the London Transport system, and it is also used, where appropriate, for much of London Transport's general typographical publicity.

ABCDEFGHIJKLMNOPQRSTUVWXYZ1234567890
abcdefghijklmnopqrstuvwxyz &£.,:;'-""!?()*

"fill in" through over-inking and which would print well on papers of varying quality were in demand by the commercial printer of the late 'twenties.

Edward Johnston, Gill's early mentor in matters of lettering, designed a sans-serif alphabet for the London Underground, where it is still widely used. He based his designs on a geometrically standardized rendering of the characters, and aimed at securing maximum legibility in a variety of weights and sizes. Elegance and abstract ideas of what was "beautiful" in letters took   *60 point Gill Sans*

ABCDEFGHIJKL MNOPQRSTUV WXYZabcdefgh ijklmnopqrstuv wxyz

Gill Sans Serif 60-point

second place to visibility and simplicity. The Johnston alphabet (see page 54) has been compared with Gill Sans and some have said that it is essentially the same alphabet as Gill designed, but there are obvious differences between the two. Gill made this point in a letter in January 1940 when he wrote that Johnston's letter "was designed primarily for station name boards, and only later became a printing type, whereas the Monotype sans-serif was designed first of all for typography, and moreover for machine punch-cutting". This does appear so when we trace Gill Sans through its typographic variants – bold, italic and display faces – and its range of sizes. What Johnston's Underground lettering and Gill Sans *do* have in common is their clean, spare, efficient, yet by no means over-"mechanical" appearance. Neither is lacking in grace nor the qualities which Gill once called "musical" when describing well-formed letters.

Johnston was modest in the public statements he made about his sans-serif. His daughter, Priscilla Johnston, makes little of the distinction between Johnston's sans and Gill's in her preface to Heather Child's edition of Johnston's *Formal Penmanship & Other Papers* (Lund Humphries, 1971) saying, "The [Johnston] block letter was designed for the Underground Railways and was a private type for their use only. When, a few years later, Eric Gill designed what was virtually the same alphabet 'owing', as he told Johnston, 'all its goodness to your Underground letter', and it became generally available under the name Gill Sans, its success was meteoric and its influence world wide." It is understandable that a lettering artist should glide over the very real problems of translating a "standardized" letterform such as Johnston's into a type family, but it is going rather too far to imply that Gill Sans was simply Johnston's alphabet under another name. The differences are sufficiently marked to show that Gill made important departures from the Johnston design which had much to do with the suitability of Gill Sans as a printing type. Whether Gill could, or would, have designed his sans in the way he did without Johnston's example and encouragement earlier on is a matter for speculation. Gill was less calligraphically-orientated at this time than Johnston was and, as his engraved work and signwriting shows, fully capable of creating a classically-inspired sans-serif.

Gill (in the letter quoted above) said of the letterforms that it seemed desirable they should be "as much as possible mathematically measurable, and as little reliance as possible should be placed on the sensibility of the draughtsman and others concerned in this machine facture. Thus the cap E has equal arms and the middle one is as near as possible to the middle, and so throughout". Gill did not give due credit, in this, to the "draughtsmen and others" who helped to perfect Gill Sans, but he did add that he did not think there was much to choose between Gill Sans and Johnston sans, though "I do think the alterations I made might be said to be an improvement from the point of view of modern production" – Gill as an advocate of "modern production"! This has proved hard to swallow by many who took Gill's other medicines without complaint. The ambivalence was present in almost everything Gill said about types and typography. It seemed as though he was arguing with himself at times.

Originally, both Gill and Johnston had been approached by Frank Pick for the London Transport lettering experiment, but Gill left the job to Johnston. Both men, so much at one in matters of design and both possessing the skill needed to carry out the work, would certainly have discussed the sans-serif challenge in detail, and Gill may be assumed to have agreed with Johnston that, if a sans-serif alphabet was what was wanted, it should be one which was rooted in the classic proportions of roman.

Gill Sans is not, in fact, purely a mechanically drawn design at all, though

✻ MEETING ¶ FEDERATION OF MASTER PRINTERS

BLACKPOOL

PUBLICITY AND

SELLING CONGRESS

 on Monday, 21st May, 1928

at the Imperial Hydro Hotel

at 2.30 p.m.

ANNUAL

Gill Sans was introduced in a design by Stanley Morison for the BFMP Congress of 1925. Many of the Master Printers were shocked by its "modern" appearance

Drawings for Gill Sans
italic

its effect on paper is of extreme regularity. It is a "visible" and uncomplicated letter (". . . they don't half stare at you – a fine test for astigmatism" wrote Gill after experimenting with "simple block letters" by cutting them out of paper and sticking them on a black background). The alphabet used by Gill for his typeface has many subtle variations of stress in the italic to vary the monotony of geometrically based letters and only in the heavy versions is there any sense of assertiveness. Gill showed the economy of an assured crafts-man who knew a short cut when he saw one and standardized the basic shapes of such letters as C, O, G and Q (see page 55).

There have been sans-serif faces which display more variations of stroke widths than Gill's (notably Adrian Frutiger's Univers, a successful present-day sans-serif) and which go further in avoiding the tendency of sans-serif types to become monotonous and, on some papers, to "dazzle" the reader, but it is my opinion that any sans-serif type can achieve only marginal success in this direction, and that roman remains most suited to large quantities of text. Serifs establish a base-line and delimit the top half of the letters, pro-viding subtle "guide lines" along which the reader's eyes can travel. Further-more, though the stress of old-face romans is vertical, the variations of stroke-width and the serifs all contribute to a horizontal movement of the eyes, whereas sans-serif types never seem to avoid a vertical or "up and down" movement. Circumstances can alter typographic solutions, however, and there can be no hard and fast rules. Gill did not seem to think of his sans as a suitable book face, but it was unquestionably an improvement on the general run of sans-serif types generally available for jobbing work, and its wide range of weights and sizes made it extremely versatile and a popular face throughout the 'thirties. It could well be that Gill Sans is due for a revival when we have got over the present fashion for elaborate typefaces resurrected from Victorian days.

The *Encyclopaedia of Typefaces* (4th edition, 1970) gives the following range

DAILY WORKER

An early use of a Gill Sans letter for a newspaper title-piece

Gill's notes on this condensed version of his Sans and (above opposite) on the drafts of an extra bold ("double elefans" he called it) show his continuing involvement with derivations from the original design

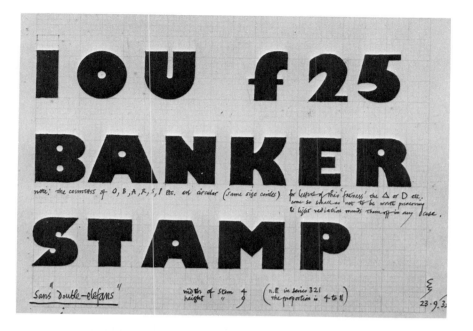

I O U £25
BANKER
STAMP

note: the counters of O, B, A, R, S, I etc. ate circular (same size circles) for letters of this 'fatness' the A or D etc.
come so small as not to be worth preserving
& lighter radiation rounds them off in any case.

"Sans double-elefans"   width of stem   4   (n.B. in series 321
height 4   9   the proportion is 4 to 11)   23·9·3

REDUCTION of HOURS
There will be a house meeting on Thursday at 5.35 in
the Men's Room, Pitt Building, to consider the new
arrangement of hours to
come into force on Sept. I.

E. A. CRUTCHLEY

10 Aug. 1937

*After cutting as Gill
Kayo the extra bold had
been somewhat
improved, but Gill
himself still did not like
it much*

for the Gill Sans family: Gill Sans Light, Gill Sans, Gill Sans Medium, Gill Sans Medium Condensed, Gill Extra Bold, Gill Kayo (or Sans Ultrabold), and six display types derived from the Gill letters, Gill Cameo, Gill Cameo Ruled, Gill Shadow Titling, Gill Shadow No 1 and Gill Sans Shadow Line. Gill called the Extra Bold and Kayo versions "absurd misconceptions" and disowned these, together with the display faces which he did not design, though he certainly "played about" as he said with the original sans-serif alphabet in its pure form and there are drawings which show some letters of a version which he jokingly called "double elefans" to demonstrate the "maximum fattening" which the typeface could stand. It is an unattractive letter and one which it is impossible to imagine Gill taking seriously, though Extra Bold was cut as Series 442 by The Monotype Corporation, without the ugly cap S and the figure 2 seen in Gill's draft. "Maximum fattening" also meant some extremely small "nicks" in such letters as the lower-case v, w, x and y, which could easily fill in with ink, particularly on poor quality papers.

Gill retained a proprietorial interest in all the derivations from Gill Sans which appeared during his lifetime. His technical criticisms of Gill Shadow appear on notes which he made on a proof of a trial cutting dated 22 December 1920. It is difficult to be sure whether the Gill Sans Bold Extra Condensed alphabet, which appeared as Series 468, was Gill's own work. Robert Harling allowed adverse criticism of this type to appear in the quarterly *Typography*, which he was then editing, and, in May 1938, he wrote to Gill suggesting improvements. The letters suggests that Gill himself had already expressed some dissatisfaction with the face for Mr Harling agrees with Gill that it is "a ridiculously narrow letter for its weight" but adds, "I do feel that, within these limitations, a new and better lower case a d e f l m n p r could have been evolved." Gill replied that any improvement "depends on the Articulate Judgement of the Reader, and Incidentally on the author himself . . . it is the book buyer and not the publisher who ought to Rebel at Starveling Types on the one hand and Freakish Novelties on the Other", a rare instance of acknowledgement by Gill that the reader's judgement on typeforms need be noted or trusted!

Gill took his advisory rôle in The Monotype Corporation very seriously and it would be remarkable indeed had he not had his say in typefaces which bore his name. Yet there are cuttings of a book advertisement in *The Observer* which show a sort of Gill Sans Extra Bold with truly grotesque malformations (a cap E lacking the middle bar, a cap A without a counter, etc) which Gill would surely have condemned.

In its familiar guises Gill Sans has more than one root, though Johnston's

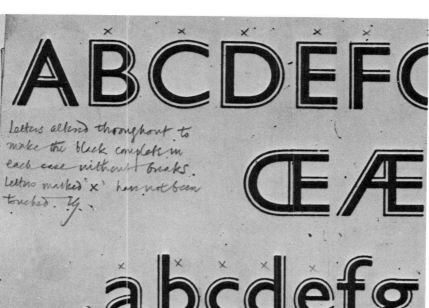

Part of Gill's revisions for Gill Inline and (below) Gill Shadow, both derived from his Gill Sans

influence was certainly present. Long before the type was designed he had produced drawn lettering considerably finer than the crude "block letters" used for signwriting and fascia lettering in that time. Gill regarded block letters as being entirely suited to signs but, at this period when, as he says in his *Autobiography*, he was going "up and down the country" executing commissions for fascias and the like, he had not encountered the special problems of designing a typeface for machine production and mechanical typesetting, nor given any thought to the type which Morison had in mind when he proposed the design of a sans-serif to Gill. Morison would undoubtedly have seen the neat and lively sans-serif which Gill executed in the fascia of Douglas Cleverdon's bookshop in Bristol. The shop was destroyed by bombing during the last war. Gill made the fascia letters with evident enjoyment in their puriyt and in his ability to make them interesting in spite of their simplicity. This was by no means "showcard" lettering, nor is Gill Sans "mechanistic" in any exact sense.

Morison was obviously pleased with Gill Sans and admired it immensely. In an internal memorandum dated 18 February 1931, he took up the cause of Gill Sans against some German critics with characteristic brusqueness: "In 1921 a tribe of German artists came here for the first time after the war, and wallowed in this Johnston sans-serif [the Johnston "Underground" letters], went back to their country and began doing just such faces as Johnston's, only of course, not quite the same." Erbar brought out his sans in 1922 and "the next thing of any importance to appear in Europe was the Gill which was cut in 1927". Later in the memorandum Morison himself spikes the guns of anybody who accuses Gill of making simply a "mechanical" letter: "The Gill type is not made in accordance with any philosophical conceptions whatever, but is a *design* intended to be satisfactory to the eyes of people who have been accustomed to what are in this country regarded as good models. These sound models have a geometrical basis, but the geometry is by no means rigidly applied." The same, of course, could be said of a classic roman! But, as Johnston's sans was, Gill's is an alphabet which could, if necessary, be copied by a signwriter to provide a good standard letter and it was adopted by the London and North Eastern Railway company at the instigation of the publicity manager, C. G. G. Dandridge, for what *The Monotype Recorder* (Vol. XXXII No 4, Winter 1933) called "a gigantic letter standardization". For this purpose 72 point Gill Sans Titling, Series 231 was cut in three sizes to create the basis from which a range of sizes could be derived by signwriters.

There is a (to me) curiously touching photograph of Gill standing next to The Royal Scot after having "painted and affixed with his own hands" the nameplate.

JOANNA

"I AM COMING ROUND BY DEGREES TO CONSIDER MYSELF CAPABLE of designing a fount of type, so it's all right and all difficulties can be got over," Gill wrote to Morison after Gill Sans had been launched. The fount of type he had in mind may not have been Joanna for he was still thinking along mechanical composition lines so far as The Monotype Corporation was concerned and Joanna was conceived as a type for fine limited edition work – the opposite, in most respects, to the *raison d'être* of Gill Sans. Joanna was designed in 1930 and engraved and cast by H. W. Caslon & Co at the Caslon Letter Foundry (now Stephenson Blake). It was intended for use in the print shop which he set up on commercial lines with his pupil and son-in-law René Hague, which became Gill's first and only venture into printing on his own account.

His step in designing a type and then commissioning a foundry to cut and cast it was unusual, but his reasons were clear. In the words of a leaflet produced by the founders but fairly certainly using Gill's own words, the new type was to be "completely *normal* in the form and details of all the characters, with all unnecessary embellishments omitted, being at the same time a design that would lend itself to satisfactory production by 'present day methods'". This suggests that Gill had already had it in mind that Joanna could be made widely available.

Here again, however, Gill was ambiguous in what he said about the type in a letter to the *Publishers Circular* in 1935. If by "present day methods" of type production he meant mechanical methods he would seem to contradict himself when he wrote, "My Joanna type was not designed to facilitate machine punch-cutting. Not at all. Machines can do practically anything. The question isn't what they *can* do but what they *should*. It is clear that machine products are best when they are plain. Machine-made ornament is nauseating. Assuming the serif is not an ornamental but a useful addition to letters (especially in book faces) the Joanna is an attempt to design a book face free from all fancy business . . . I only claim it is on the right lines for machine production." Which may be taken either as an example of Gill putting his money on "each way", or of his propensity for making debating points whenever the opportunity presented itself. I prefer to believe the latter to be the case, and that Gill was merely asserting the craftsmans' dominance over the machine, even when the machine of necessity came into the picture.

Joanna was cast at first in only two sizes, 8 point and 12 point, with the smaller 12 point capitals made with a view to obtaining a good uniform colour on the page. "Generally speaking," Gill wrote, "caps are heavier than lower-case, and as a result stand out all over the page. By using Joanna small caps in the general body of the text and ordinary caps only for headings and initials of paragraphs a uniformity of colour can be obtained".

Of particular interest in the Joanna family is the italic, a letter so distinctive as to be easily recognized even by non-typographers. The roman is lightly shaded, reticent and efficient though, for today's economies of space in most book pages, its set width is perhaps over generous. Gill's *Essay on Typography* (see Chapter 5) was set in 12 point Joanna for its first edition of 500 copies and the typeface was retained for later editions. Joanna was cut by The Monotype Corporation in 1938 for Messrs J. M. Dent in a range of sizes from 8

Drawings by Gill for
Joanna

point to 36 point roman and italic and was made available to the trade in 1958.

From the start Gill had put forward the "simplicity" of the face as its prime virtue, leaving others to discover that such simplicity is achieved only by the most artful means. In a booklet, *A Specimen of Three Book Types* which Hague & Gill printed in 1934, Joanna is said to be "a truly machine-made letter" (whatever that means!) and "in no sense a fancy letter".

Joanna italic is such a delightful letter — "pleasing, almost gay" thought Robert Harling — that it can conveniently be used to elucidate some points about italic generally. Morison argued in *The Fleuron* ,Vol 5 (1926), that an italic type should be an "inclined roman" and seems only partially to have convinced Gill of this in Joanna where the italic forms show minor differences from the roman. In a few letters Gill has preferred calligraphic forms. There were originally no Joanna italic caps, the roman capitals being entirely appropriate to the italic due to the latter's very slight incline, a feature which has made Joanna italic appropriate to much larger areas of setting than are usually thought desirable for italic types.

Although italics have been familiar in print since first used by Aldus Manutius in 1500 in Venice (mainly as a device for getting a larger quantity of text into a given space) it has rarely been successful in continuous text settings. The slope to the right adds, to my mind, nothing to legibility and is a leftover from the rightward slope natural to penformed letters. Italic is usually encountered with roman where contrast is needed.

Italic, as its name implies, is derived from the cursive, pen formed scripts which were brought to a high degree of style by Italian calligraphers in the fifteenth century. It is therefore a letter historically different from roman insofar as it originated not as an engraved letter but as a pen-written one. The italic slope is, strictly speaking, irrelevant to the needs of type, though it was seized on as a convenient way of providing a distinguishable text variant of roman. Historically speaking, italic is not a "sloped roman" in spite of Morison's edict, and its character resides more in the flowing (cursive) and rounded qualities of penformed script. In designing his Joanna italic Gill was well aware of the danger of too much slope and, "inclined roman" or not, the face is among Gill's most felicitous creations. It is particularly well shown in *The Sonnets of William Shakespeare*, edited by Margaret Flower, in the Cassell edition of 1933.

In his essay in *Alphabet & Image* Robert Harling wrote: "In the Joanna italic, each character, judged separately, is affected, and should thus prove obtrusive and beyond the pale. The c and e are most casually curved; the a is too like the o; the w is too wide for the set of the remaining characters in the alphabet; the downstroke of the y is too sudden, and the g is too exquisite and seizes too swiftly on the eye. Yet the type in the mass has a congenial unity which defies the laws of optics and the dicta of pundits. Here is none of that mannered affectation engaged upon by, say the designer of Monotype Pastonchi, mannerisms which are quickly wearying and tiresome to the reader. Here is no poet turning his dilletante's attention to the problems of type design, but a master of letter-forms engaged on a pleasurable task for his own occasions."

At the time when this was written Joanna was still the property of Hague & Gill. It was not strictly a private press type because the firm was not a private press, but it was a founder's type and existed for many years as a type more enjoyed by typographical cognoscenti than by the ordinary reader. It is a useful exercise to compare the Caslon founts of Joanna with the Monotype

Drawings for Joanna italic, a "jewel-like" letter with a decidedly calligraphic g

version cut for machine composition, and to discover whether the exigencies of machine punch-cutting have to any significant extent deprived Joanna of its spontaneity. To this writer's eye it has not. A specimen setting immediately convinces the reader of its respectable antecedents among the classic book-faces. Joanna is as Gill wanted it to be – a "decent" typeface without quirks. Though first used to set the first 500 copies of the *Essay on Typography* in 1931, its most splendid showing was in The Aldine Bible, New Testament, published by Dent between 1934 and 1936.

In a booklet, *The Story of Joanna* by James Moran, reprinted from *Book Design & Production*, and written in 1958 when Monotype Joanna was about to become available to anybody owning a Monotype machine, the problems of using a "house" type in the wider world of publishing are noted in connection with The Aldine Bible. "The setting was carried out in Joanna type at Hague & Gill's printing shop, but the type was sent on to the Temple Press (now the Aldine Press) at Letchworth in Hertfordshire for machining on Miehle presses. Dent's returned the type for distribution when formes were machined, and the type was used for new setting of succeeding pages until the completion of the project. The type was 8 point and 12 point roman and 12 point italic (lower case only). Dent's were provided with a fount of each to make any necessary corrections. Hague & Gill then ordered 24 point capitals from Caslon's, but only those required by the Aldine Bible for the initials making divisions into chapters. Thus not the full alphabet was provided – E, U, X, Y and Z were not made, and, as has been noted from the original leaflet, there were no italic capitals." A good example, then, of collaboration between people determined to achieve a typographical *chef d'oeuvre* and the factory methods needed to produce it.

Dent's ordered Monotype matrices of Joanna 11 point in 1938. The fount, Series 478, included an italic lower-case, italic comma and italic caps for A, I and O only. In 1942 Dent's acquired Monotype matrices for 18 and 24 point Joanna caps. Thereafter a number of books published by Dent's were printed in Joanna 478 11 point on 12 point body and 11 on 13 point. Joanna thus emerged in a gradual way from its more exclusive origins. It could be said, therefore, that Joanna was a Gill windfall for Monotype, though Gill was closely involved in the redesign of the italic before it was recut for Monotype.

SOLUS

SOLUS HAS LED A SOMEWHAT SHADOWED AND SOLITARY LIFE among Gill's type designs. It was cut (as Series 276) for The Monotype Corporation in 1929 and followed Perpetua which, in some respects, it resembles. The year 1929 was prolific for Gill types. Apart from Solus he designed the Golden Cockerel type (see page 77) and was at work on the Greek version of his Perpetua roman. Solus appears to have been an attempt to provide a type with "Egyptian" characteristics without making the slab serifs so aggressive as to put it out of court. Gill was, by this time, not insensitive to the wider requirements of typefaces other than book faces and the "Egyptians" were then much admired by advertising people and some commercial printers. Solus, however, was a special case, a commission via Monotype from what the Gill commemorative issue of *The Monotype Recorder* reticently calls "a department of state". This was the Empire Marketing Board, which had taken the enlightened step of accepting The Monotype Corporation's offer of its, and Gill's, co-operation in creating a new typeface for its publications. The Gill letter was to suit the dignity of the Board and the gravity of its public utterances. But politics outside the sphere of type design intervened and the Board's plans for a Gill type did not get far ahead.

Solus is referred to among Gill's "experiments" in the Gill commemorative issue of *The Monotype Recorder* which, to my mind, sells it rather short. It is a light "Egyptian" of the kind which Gill had included in a book of model alphabets which he drew for Douglas Cleverdon and which, in a letter to Gill in July 1928, Stanley Morison had said "would make a very good fount". He had also said, in the same letter, that he was "a little nervous about the serifs", adding: "I like them very much indeed, and would propose having entirely flat, unbracketed terminations, very much in the style of the accompanying proof of series 135; but as far as the ascenders are concerned, I think a simple, and not a double serif would be best."

Solus fully met Morison's request for a fount of "a definitely light, blonde colour; the kind of letter which should look exceedingly well with intaglio plates". The first designs were on an 18 point scale and the smaller sizes were "worked over" in the manner described on page 24. The serifs are so unexaggerated as to deceive the casual glance into accepting them as a conventional roman. They are, unlike many of the more popular "Egyptians", well-integrated with the letters and do not strike the eye as forcibly as do those of, say Clarendon or Monotype Rockwell, both popular "Egyptian" faces: Gill might recognize a trend, but he was incapable of over-emphasis. In the case of Solus it may well be that Gill's subtlety went unnoticed, or simply that Solus was so much like Perpetua that its distinguishing characteristics were lost to the casual eye. These include, apart from the serifs, differing forms of the lower-case p and q in Gill's original design which were later altered after "realistic consultations with the technicians of the [Monotype] type drawing office".

There is a 48 point display face and 18, 14 and 12 point text sizes, but no italic. In its 48 point size the individuality of Solus is easily discerned. It has great regularity and, compared with Gill's romans, a fairly narrow set width. Yet, in the final analysis of a type which is usually subjective, one must admit that Solus is not an altogether successful compromise between the rhythmic grace of a roman titling such as Perpetua Titling and the strength of the better "Egyptians", which tends more towards a "mechanical" letter than does roman. The fact that, when Solus was made generally available by Monotype, there were "Egyptians" a-plenty — Beton, Karnak, Memphis, and Rockwell were already cut — has left Solus in an eclipse from which it shows little sign of emerging.

The Solus type, Series No. 276 was designed by Eric Gill for The Monotype Corporation in 1929.

The type is available in 48-pt display, in the 18-pt and 14-pt, and in this 12-point text size. No italic fount was designed to accompany the roman.

ARIES

ARIES IS NOT WELL-KNOWN AMONG THE GILL TYPE DESIGNS. He designed it for the exclusive use of the Stourton Press, a private press owned by B. Fairfax Hall, in 1932, a year after the Stourton Press was started. It was cut and founded by the Caslon Letter Foundry, though it was not seen until some years after its founding. The type has the elegance which one gets used to anticipating in a Gill design and the italic has a calligraphic quality removed from a "sloped roman", though not so inspired as Joanna italic. The roman, cast in 18 point, 14 point and 10 point, had its greatest moment of glory when used for the magnificent *Catalogue of Chinese Pottery and Porcelain in the Collection of Sir Percival David Bt*, which was published by the Stourton Press in an edition of 630 copies in 1934, on hand-made paper and bound in silk. The italic was used by the Stourton Press, also in 1934, to print Marlowe's *Hero and Leander*.

Aries has sufficient similarity to Morison's Times New Roman, which appeared in 1932, to suggest at least the possibility that Morison may have studied and learned from Gill's designs, though Aries is unquestionably a more consciously noble type and, in the 18 point size, the lapidary quality of the type shows its specialized character. The serifs slope in the lower-case, and the set width is as generous as befits its private press purpose.

It has been suggested that the *Catalogue of Chinese Pottery and Porcelain* was the one and only appearance of Aries, but this is incorrect. Mr Fairfax Hall went to South Africa after the Second World War and returned to London in 1961 where he continued printing. The Press still owns the punches and matrices of Aries, which it casts on its own pivotal caster. Mr Fairfax Hall is known to have given some of the type to the University of Cape Town before leaving South Africa and it would be unusual had the University not experimented with it.

Aries is an extremely harmonious type, more colourful on the page than Joanna or Solus and with greater stroke contrast than either of them. It is a type which "lets the light in" well.

A rare showing of Aries
in an edition by The
Stourton Press of
Marlowe's "Hero and
Leander"

And beat from thence, have lighted there againe.
About her necke hung chaines of peble stone,
Which lightned by her necke, like Diamonds shone.
She ware no gloves, for neither sunne nor wind
Would burne or parch her hands, but to her mind,
Or warme or coole them, for they tooke delite
To play upon those hands, they were so white.
Buskins of shels all silvered, used she,
And brancht with blushing corall to the knee;
Where sparrowes pearcht, of hollow pearle and gold,
Such as the world would woonder to behold:
Those with sweet water oft her handmaid fils,
Which as shee went would cherupe through the bils.

Hero's excellent beauty Some say, for her the fairest Cupid pyn'd,
And looking in her face, was strooken blind.
But this is true, so like was one the other,
As he imagyn'd Hero was his mother.
And oftentimes into her bosome flew,
About her naked necke his bare armes threw.
And laid his childish head upon her brest,
And with still panting rockt, there tooke his rest.
So lovely faire was Hero, Venus Nun,
As nature wept, thinking she was undone;
Because she tooke more from her than she left,
And of such wondrous beautie her bereft:
Therefore in signe her treasure suffred wracke,

6

JUBILEE

THERE ARE PLENTY OF LESS ATTRACTIVE AND MORE IDIO-syncratic display typefaces than Jubilee. Gill worked, on and off, with Jubilee and Bunyan during 1934. The former was designed for the Sheffield foundry of Stephenson Blake and cast in 10 sizes from 10 to 72 point "for advertising and general work" and, in Stephenson Blake's leaflet on the type, it is said to be "by the eminent sculptor Mr Eric Gill". In the same brochure Gill wrote: "In deference to demand an alphabet of capitals has been designed to 'go' with it; but there is not properly a capital alphabet for this type of letter and it would be better to follow the ancient practice of using roman capitals for initials." The ambiguity of a type intended for advertising and general work, but in the use of which ancient practices were recommended, was caught by a critic in the printing supplement of *World's Press News*, a trade publication, who commented, "Jubilee may be described as a special jobbing face, a half-black. It suggests a design by a fifteenth-century founder who had been studying ancient roman inscriptions, or who, by some miracle, had been able to project himself for a moment into the twentieth century."

Nobody, it seemed, was quite sure what Jubilee was for and the type certainly stands in some distinction from the rest of Gill's output in being an attempt, apparently deliberate, to provide an "unusual" letter. At first it was to be called Cunard, but the Jubilee of the coronation of King George V and Queen Mary in 1935 must have been too good an opportunity to miss when naming a typeface which appeared for that year.

One interesting facet of the design is not detectable from the type itself: it is the technique used by Gill for making some of the finished drawings of the type. They are not, in fact, drawings at all, being cut from white board in the form of stencils and placed over a black background. What prompted Gill to do this? The type can be roughly classified as "calligraphic" insofar as it displays the kind of serif which a calligrapher could make with a broad-nibbed pen. Wolfgang Kehr ("Eric Gill als Schriftkünstler" in *Archiv für Geschiche des Buchwesens*) sees, in Jubilee, a harking back to Edward Johnston's influence on Gill in that Johnston took tenth century scripts as models for his foundation hand. But — and in this the confusion of period which the World's

THIS new Cunard Design is based upon the writing of 15th Century Italian Scribes. Pen Lettering such as was used in old illuminated manuscripts has always been a basis for type design, but never has the beauty of the original characters been preserved so well as in this fine series, which conforms with the accepted conventions of design and will at once commend itself to every discerning user of type

Specimen setting of Jubilee (then called Cunard) which shows that it was intended to be a calligraphically-inspired face. The initial letter is probably not Gill's

Press News writer found is understandable – Jubilee is a printing type, unmistakably, and Gill had moved appreciably away from the freedom of the calligrapher so that the type seems both mannered and restricted. The lower-case has a certain "olde worlde" charm, but the capitals seem altogether too domineering.

Gill's judgement may have been swayed by the commercial success of Gill Sans to the extent of believing – or being persuaded – that he could fill a need for a durable display type. Jubilee was much revised before being cut in three large sizes initially, 72, 60 and 48 point.

A display type should be more striking, more "illustrative" and, if possible, more memorable than its text equivalent in order to carry out its different typographical tasks. While he may have recognized this, Gill was not the sort of man who studied the ways of the market-place with much sympathy or understanding. Robert Harling calls Jubilee "unfortunate"; *The Monotype Recorder*'s Eric Gill Commemorative issue ignores it altogether (as well as not mentioning Bunyan). Jubilee should not be confused with the typeface of the same name designed by Walter Tracy for Linotype.

GOLDEN COCKEREL

OTHER THAN ARIES, THE TYPE WHICH GILL DESIGNED FOR Robert Gibbings of the Golden Cockerel Press is his only venture into a specifically private press type. It was founded by the Caslon foundry in 1929 and an italic, but no italic caps, was cut two years later. Robert Gibbings' private press was at its most influential in the 1930s. It specialized in fine editions and, particularly in books containing wood-engravings, with which the type is particularly harmonious, having the strength to stand on a page with the contrasting black and white and general weightiness of colour of most wood-engravings. Gill's own wood-engravings, including some very beautiful initial letters, were used by the press.

The type follows Perpetua. The italic is shown well in *The Songs and Poems of Dryden*, published by the Golden Cockerel Press in 1959. It is now in the possession of Thomas Yoseloff who bought it from the Press in 1959. The roman was first used in *The Four Gospels*, printed by Gibbings in 1931, and containing a fine series of Gill wood-engravings. Here we may also see the grace and ebullience of Gill's foliate decoration, reflected in his foliated initials based on the Gill Sans titling.

The Golden Cockerel Type was to be cast in 14 and 18 point, and Gill's drafts were made after photographic enlargements had been prepared to 18 point size of Jenson roman and Caslon, which he then worked over, making his own alterations and appreciably changing the originals, to make the type a crisper and more "modern" version of the classic faces. An italic was cut in 14 point only. The Golden Cockerel type was first used for A. E. Coppard's *The Hundredth Story* in 1930.

And they said unto him, In Bethlehem of Judea: for thus it
is written by the prophet;
  And thou, Bethlehem, in the land of Juda,
  Art not the least among the princes of Juda:
  For out of thee shall come a Governor,
  That shall rule my people Israel.
Then Herod, when he had privily called the wise men, in-
quired of them diligently what time the star appeared.
And he sent them to Bethlehem; and said, Go and search
diligently for the young child; and when ye have found him,
bring me word again, that I may come and worship him also.
When they had heard the king, they departed: & lo, the star,
which they saw in the east, went before them, till it came
and stood over where the young child was. When they saw
the star, they rejoiced with exceeding great joy. And when
they were come into the house, they saw the young child
with Mary his mother, and fell down, and worshipped him:

6

The Golden Cockerel type was a private press type suited for use with wood engravings on the page. It is seen here in "The Four Gospels" printed by the Golden Cockerel Press in 1931

BUNYAN

TWO YEARS AFTER ARIES APPEARED, HAGUE & GILL, PRINTERS, were asked to design and print a new edition of Laurence Sterne's *A Sentimental Journey* for the Limited Editions Club of New York, and it was there that Bunyan made its first appearance. The type stands in family relationship to Gill's other roman types, Perpetua, Joanna and Aries, with its austere simplicity allied to a stylish classicism which makes Bunyan, in Robert Harling's view, "a contemporary classic — one of Gill's most pleasing designs". On Hague & Gill's writing paper there exists, in the Monotype collection, some detailed "notes for the designer" which clearly indicate Gill's thoughts about the form which the type should take. They are as follows: "1 Width. The total width of the lower case characters (a – z excluding ligatures, & æ œ) shd be the same as Joanna – 11¼ ems of its own body (see exhibit A). 2 Weight – not heavier in effect than Perpetua. 3 Proportions of ascender & descender: the same as Joanna. Capitals same height as in Perpetua. 4 Thick & thin – not so much as Perpetua (see exhibit B) but more than Joanna. The thickest parts of letters not to be thicker than Perpetua. 5 Serifs. I don't know. In some ways I'd like Joanna ones; but if they are this sort .. I'd like them not so frightfully sharp as Perpetua. If you had Joanna ones rounded on the inside wd they become blobs .. Probably not, as big as 14 point. 6 Exhibit C shows Joanna about 14 point. The Bunyan 14 pt will be made smaller on the body than this, the same size as Caslon 14. 7 The Italic – to be designed more for difference than Joanna but not so much slope as to make it bad when used by itself. Italic to have its own caps."

These notes are undated, and what Gill's "exhibits" were is difficult to ascertain exactly. But they show, apart from Gill's first ideas about Bunyan, the early stage at which he was ready to bring Morison and the other people at The Monotype Corporation into a discussion on a new type, and also that Gill was satisfied to use his own earlier romans, Perpetua and Joanna, as touchstones for later designs; this one proved to be his last.

Some confusion may be caused by the fact that Bunyan appeared as a "private" type from Monotype in 1934, and, after Gill's death, Linotype produced Pilgrim, announced as "a type face based on a design by Eric Gill" which is, in effect, the same type face, though the Linotype Pilgrim has an italic, not provided with Bunyan. It was first used in a posthumously-published edition of Gill's own *Jerusalem Diary* in 1953. Gill did some preliminary work on a Bunyan italic which was never cut. Though the Linotype italic is good, Perpetua italic (Felicity) or even Joanna italic with Bunyan seems to the writer unobjectionable, though the latter is of somewhat heavy colour in contrast to the lightness of Bunyan. In either version, Bunyan or Pilgrim, the type is one which repays study by anyone wishing to make a subjective assessment of Gill's contribution to the roman type letter. It was — as was his Golden Cockerel type (see page 77) — another attempt to design a face suited to the fine book and, in its reticent way, succeeds well, being light in colour, even in shading and generous in form.

This may be the moment to say something about Gill's unique ability to show the roman alphabet's capacity for variety and versatility within its own strict canon of forms. A careful comparison of Gill's roman types demonstrates the minute changes in spatial and other relationships, in the serif forms and in their weight on the page, which contribute so much to the individuality

A Sentimental Journey

¶ The type from which this edition of 'A Sentimental Journey' will be printed is a new 14-pt Roman designed by Eric Gill and cut by H. W. Caslon and Co. Ltd. ¶ The paper has been made by hand by J. Barcham Green and Son, Hayle Mill, Maidstone. ¶ The 8 Illustrations are etched in copper by Denis Tegetmeier. ¶ The size of the book is Demy 4to, about 150 pages. ¶ The binding will be in full linen with gilt top. ¶ The printers are Hague and Gill, High Wycombe, England.

Bunyan, printed in this specimen by Gill's own printing firm. Note his preference (as in the *Essay on Typography*) for the paragraph sign in place of indentation which exists within the classical traditionalism of his alphabets. It is much more difficult to make a fresh approach to classic letterforms, as Gill did, than to set out to create "new" typefaces to meet a demand for novelty. What we can admire in Perpetua, Joanna, Bunyan, Gill Sans, Solus, Aries and other types is that all of them, in different ways, are specific "answers" to typographical questions concerning the appropriateness of a type as it functions.

It is to such qualities that we look to decide whether a type is "readable" in continuous text, or appropriate in different surroundings, such as on a title page or in an advertisement. There are many typefaces, and people – including typographers – sometimes wonder why there should have been so many. Yet those which are memorable, which catch the eye by dramatic gestures or strong individuality are rarely those which stand the test of time. They are not meant to. Print, in many of its manifestations, is ephemeral enough to accept the transitory qualities of some types but, in a text type and on the scale of a bookface, eccentricity or inconsistency of forms which may need a glass to detect in a specimen alphabet, become obtrusive and disturbing to the reader. A text type should, in Beatrice Warde's well-known analogy with a crystal goblet, "contain" the words without obscuring them as a glass contains a liquid, though, as with a fine glass, a fine type may subtly enhance that which it contains.

The designer of a type which is intended for text setting must recognize that he is working within traditions which have stood the test of time: that which is amusing, striking or felicitious in a few lines of displayed type will become tedious and obstructive of meaning in a text page.

POSTSCRIPT

"IF ANYONE SUGGESTED THAT ERIC GILL'S INFLUENCE HAS NOT ceased to diminish since his death, I would not be disposed to disagree," writes Robert Speaight in his biography of Gill. The point is put delicately; maybe Gill himself would have been content to have it so, as long as his work could still be seen and enjoyed for what it is rather than for what is said about it by himself or others. We are now far enough from those pre-war years to find it difficult to be concerned with the preoccupations of Gill and his contemporaries with sympathetic feeling. The arguing and debating of such problems as those which exercised Gill's pen sound far off, divided from the present by social, technical and political change. Gill was, in the modern sense of the word, "committed" and this, at least, we can understand rather better than did most of his contemporaries. He was concerned about the quality of life as he saw it. He did not write for posterity, or for literary fame, but because he wanted to draw attention to things which he felt were in need of it. His writing, therefore, had a journalistic immediacy; he tackled ideas directly and struck when the iron was hot, and he needed friction and opposition to get started. From a contemporary standpoint, though, it is hard to recall the salient issues which Gill saw as vital, though we have by no means learned all the lessons he sought to teach. Gill loved order, sanity, beauty, friendship – human qualities and spiritual values – and strove hard to uphold them: "The work I have chiefly tried to do in my life is to make a cell of good living in the chaos of our world," he said, and the sentiment is the more genuine when one knows what Gill did and said.

Only occasionally was he pessimistic, as when he wrote, in a letter to his brother Romney in 1911, "We live in the middle of chaos and at present the only forces for order are purely materialistic – therefore doomed." So the messages which Gill flashed to his time were urgent and telegraphic, not the sober reflections of a pundit nor the generalizations of the popular soothsayer but sharp reminders by a man who saw danger in the sort of society which had emerged from the industrial revolution and felt that the artist, the craftsman and the workman could help to improve it.

On the tombstone which Eric Gill carved for himself are simply the words "Pray for me / Eric Gill / Stone Carver". This is how he wanted to be remembered: the rest he left to be discovered by anybody with enough interest and curiosity to do so. This book has been concerned with but a single aspect of Gill; an activity which he took up relatively late in life and which was by no means central to him. He was proud to be called a "stone carver". In a letter to Jaques Raverat he wrote, "I am just a letter cutter who has taken to 'sculpture' . . ." and he would, no doubt, have said the same about his types. His work was with letters and what could be more natural than that he should put himself at the disposal of people who could use him? "No one," he writes in his *Autobiography*, "can say lettering is not a useful trade."

"It all goes together" has practical as well as philosophical connotations when one reviews Gill's phenomenal output in various media. The virtues of Perpetua as a type can be detected in Gill's inscriptional lettering; the cool authority of a foliated initial is reflected in the cool authority of his sculptured figures. For such reasons I recognized the problems of writing about Gill's types at the outset, and may not have avoided the danger of seeing only part of the picture. But it is a part which has not received the attention accorded his other work, and it is, I believe, an important and durable part. Recently I was in a train with someone who asked: "Does one see much of Gill's work about nowadays?" We were stopped at a station and I was able to point out of the window at a bookstall. There were the letters which Gill designed for W. H. Smith, still functioning, still admirable and, as letters will always be, mute.

Gill himself was what we might now call "a personality", though his personality was not a mask for public appearances – he made few enough of these. His enthusiasm, passionate convictions, vulnerability and, above all, his warmth echo more faintly over the years, though there are still those who can testify to these qualities in Gill. As for the rest of us, we have his letter-cutting, his types, his sculpture and his illustration to see, to admire and to use. Maybe we should re-read his words more often as a reminder of how easy it is to mislay things of value and to lose, through complacency, lethargy, and ignorance, those which were so hard to win. "We must remain content to see darkly," wrote Gill. We must also be grateful to those who sometimes saw more clearly than the rest of us.

Index

Page numbers in Italic type refer to illustrations or their captions. The names of various founts of type are listed together under the heading *Typefaces*.

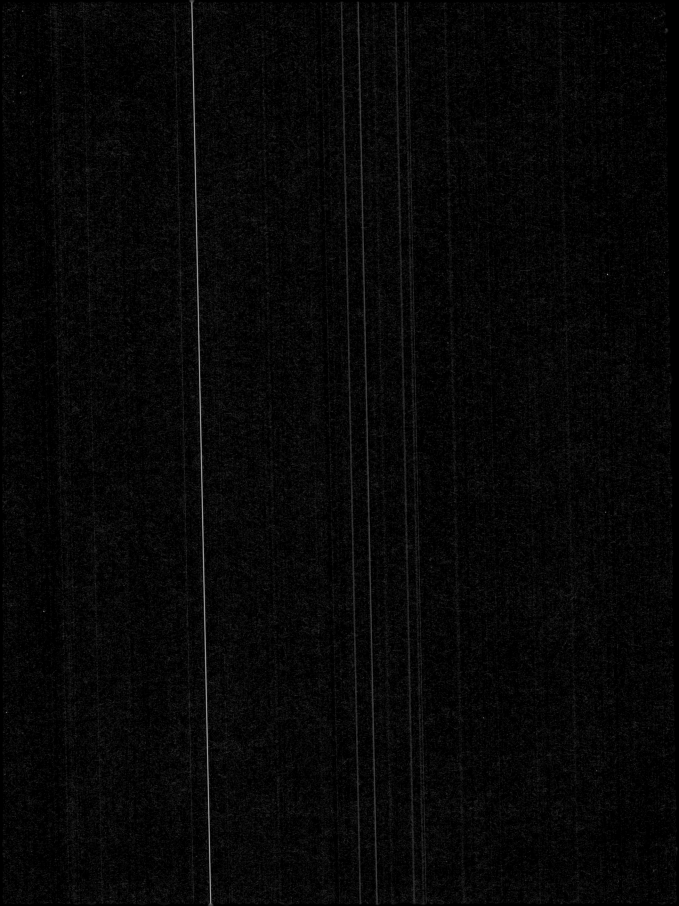